China after Jiang

China after Jiang

Edited by

Gang Lin and Xiaobo Hu

Woodrow Wilson Center Press
Washington, D.C.

Stanford University Press
Stanford, California

EDITORIAL OFFICES

Woodrow Wilson Center Press
One Woodrow Wilson Plaza
1300 Pennsylvania Avenue, N.W.
Washington, D.C. 20004
Telephone 202-691-4029
www.wilsoncenter.org

ORDER FROM

Stanford University Press
Chicago Distribution Center
11030 South Langley Avenue
Chicago, Ill. 60628
Telephone 1-800-621-2736; 773-568-1550

2 4 6 8 9 7 5 3 1

Library of Congress Cataloging-in-Publication Data

China after Jiang / edited by Gang Lin and Xiaobo Hu.
    p. cm.
Introduction / Gang Lin and Xiaobo Hu — Chinese leadership succession
to the fourth generation / Lowell Dittmer — Ideology and political
institutions for a new era / Gang Lin — The state and the private
sector in a new property rights system / Xiaobo Hu — One country, three
systems : state/society relations in post-Jiang China / Richard Madsen
— New leaders, new foreign policymaking procedures? / David Bachman.
Includes bibliographical references and index.
    ISBN 0-8047-4918-3 (Cloth : alk. paper) — ISBN 0-8047-4919-1
(Paperback : alk. paper)
1. China—Politics and government—1976– 2. Political
leadership—China. I. Lin, Gang, 1953– II. Hu, Xiaobo.
    JQ1516.C45245 2003
    320.951—dc 21
                                                    2003009479

ABOUT THE CENTER

The Center is the living memorial of the United States of America to the nation's twenty-eighth president, Woodrow Wilson. Congress established the Woodrow Wilson Center in 1968 as an international institute for advanced study, "symbolizing and strengthening the fruitful relationship between the world of learning and the world of public affairs." The Center opened in 1970 under its own board of trustees.

In all its activities the Woodrow Wilson Center is a nonprofit, nonpartisan organization, supported financially by annual appropriations from the Congress, and by the contributions of foundations, corporations, and individuals. Conclusions or opinions expressed in Center publications and programs are those of the authors and speakers and do not necessarily reflect the views of the Center staff, fellows, trustees, advisory groups, or any individuals or organizations that provide financial support to the Center.

Contents

Foreword

Scholars and journalists have already felled whole forests with both instant analyses and erudite exegeses on China's new political leadership that was introduced to the world in November 2002 during the 16th National Congress of the Chinese Communist Party. Do we, one might reasonably ask, need yet another variation on this theme? Perhaps not . . . if China is likely to be nothing more than a middling power in the new century. Perhaps not . . . if it is of little import to what is customarily called the West whether China evolves into a stable, mature, more-or-less responsible nation-state, or instead, marries its growing economic power with a well-developed sense of nationalism, liberally sprinkled with memories of national humiliation and shame, and becomes an erratic, unpredictable, capricious state with little sense of obligation to either its neighbors or its own people.

In fact, few would argue with the proposition that it behooves us in the West to develop a far better understanding of the complex tangle of energy and contradictions that is China today. And while one might begin such a quest from any number of points, the transfer of political power underway in the People's Republic—the first such transition in PRC history not occasioned by death or political crisis—is not merely a logical starting point, but also provides us with a window into other, even more basic features of the Chinese polity. *China after Jiang* is a study of far more than individual leaders or a specific Party congress. In a nice touch of irony, the authors of the essays presented here use the occasion of political elite change to get at the more fundamental institutional evolution that China must experience if it is to flourish over the long run. Underneath their analyses lies an assumption that while personalities come and go, institutions survive.

As a consequence, ideology, rule-making and -breaking, Party governance, bureaucracy, the use of state power for economic ends, questions of legitimacy, and the relationship of state to society loom large in these pages. While politics is never absent from these essays, they also encourage us to contemplate social, cultural, and economic change, as well as foreign policy. What are the linkages between ideology and institutions? How have shifts in the concept and meaning of property rights influenced

China's development? Will China's new bosses be able to perpetuate the Party's monopoly on political power by partially democratizing the Party—in effect, using democratic means to sustain a nondemocratic system of governance? In what manner will the politics of elite succession color Chinese decision making in the foreign policy and national security arenas? How does one best understand the nature of contemporary Chinese society? These are important questions that extend far beyond the usual review of China's political transition and help illustrate why this book is likely to be consulted long after most other analyses of the transfer of power have ended up in forgotten corners of largely ignored bookshelves.

This present volume is a logical and most timely follow-up to an earlier collaboration by Xiaobo Hu and Gang Lin, *Transition towards Post-Deng China* (Singapore University Press, 2001). Lin and Hu are exemplars of a younger generation of U.S. scholars—born in China, educated in the United States, and now exerting a growing influence in both U.S. classrooms and the community of China scholars. The Woodrow Wilson International Center for Scholars is extremely proud that both editors have close ties to the Center. Hu was a visiting scholar at the Center in 2001, while Lin has been a program associate with the Center's Asia Program, and the Center's principal China expert, for more than three years. It has been my privilege to work with both these scholars, and to learn from them.

These essays portray a potentially unstable China in desperate need of strong institutions to bring order and regularity to the country. Whether Hu Jintao and his "fourth-generation" colleagues will succeed in providing those institutions and their concomitant stability is one of the large question marks hovering over China's future. This admirable volume, by forcing us to think of politics as something more encompassing than mere personalities, offers the student of China a surer understanding of the present. It also makes it possible for us to speak with somewhat greater confidence about the future of what will surely be one of the great powers of the twenty-first century.

Robert M. Hathaway
Director, Asia Program
Woodrow Wilson International Center for Scholars
December 2002

Introduction

Gang Lin and Xiaobo Hu

The 16th National Congress of the Chinese Communist Party (CCP) in November 2002 commenced a new era for the People's Republic of China (PRC). Jiang Zemin's retirement and Hu Jintao's coronation as Party general secretary and PRC president initiated the first power transition in the history of the PRC that was unprompted by the death of the top leader or a political crisis.[1] But, behind closed doors, the leadership transition is far from complete. Jiang Zemin is likely to retain his political influence in the early stage of post-Jiang China. First, Jiang's seminal idea of the "Three Represents" has been enshrined in the Party constitution.[2] Second, Jiang's protégés have taken strategic posts within the Standing Committee of the Politburo, the Party's highest policymaking organ. Third, Jiang may still speak on critical policy issues through formal and informal channels. Since political power in China is highly concentrated at the top and Chinese politics still depends to a certain degree on informal politics, leadership transitions have significant implications for the country's political reform and economic transformation processes.

1

In the past, leadership transition also transformed the institutional foundations of China's political and economic power, including rules of the game, socioeconomic policies, state–society relationships, and foreign relations. How is this current transition different from previous ones? What are the fundamental principles underlying this succession or the new principles being created? What is the role of ideology? Are the new leaders likely to promote significant political reform? What is the nature of the socioeconomic environment during the transition period? What is the possible impact of this transition on China's foreign policy? This book offers a general investigation of China's gradual but profound institutional changes and their long-term impact on the country's future development.

Contributors to the following chapters go beyond one-time speculations on the likelihood of different scenarios related to the fourth generation of Chinese leadership during the transition period—for example, whether Hu Jintao will completely succeed Jiang, what Hu's ruling style will be, and so on. Rather, they focuses on rule making, rule breaking, and institutional transformation, providing a comprehensive analysis of the changing institutional foundation of Chinese politics for a long time to come.

All the chapters in this volume highlight the ongoing transformation of the institutional foundations of Chinese political and economic power. "Institutions" refer to formal structures as well as unwritten principles, rules, and norms.[3] Viewing politics as interactions among political players and between political players and institutions, this volume addresses the most urgent and profound issues immediately challenging the Chinese leadership. Contributors to this book employ a coherent theoretical approach, viewing politics as a result of interaction between political actors' self-interests and institutional constraints. Our approach emphasizes the adaptability of individuals to existing institutional arrangements as well as individuals' abilities to renovate and create new institutions to serve their ends.

This volume starts with a thorough analysis of Chinese succession politics by focusing on the transition from the third to the fourth generation of leaders. In Chapter 1, Lowell Dittmer concentrates on pre-existing and emerging rules and norms governing power succession and those shaping the structure of China's power elite. According to Dittmer, China's leadership transition is simultaneously moving along both formal and informal political tracks. Formally, the selection of ministerial, provincial, and regional military leaders proceeds with considerable transparency and modest competition. Informally, incumbents and candidates at the top level are maneuvering for power with elaborate subtlety and political opacity. With the final outcome of the power maneuvers in abeyance, Dittmer makes it clear that the political stakes for, and policy difference between, winners and losers are rather subtle. Even devout advocates of complete retirement of the entire third generation of leaders (including Jiang Zeimin, Li Peng, Zhu Rougji, Li Ruihuan, and so forth) would tolerate a continuing advisory role for Jiang Zemin. On the other hand, those with the greatest misgivings over Jiang's full retirement do not deny the need for institutional rejuvenation and eventual generational transition. As the Chinese elite structure today is no longer divided by ideology (as in the Mao era) or policy cleavages (as in the Deng era), change within the top leadership is unlikely to bring about a dramatic policy shift in the short term. Indeed, the Chinese leadership understands very well that political instability and policy uncertainty are counterproductive to China's economic development, and are therefore unappealing. The existence of informal politics has contributed to a succession syndrome with numerous, and often self-contradictory, speculations.[4] Dittmer demonstrates that throughout the reform decades, Chinese leadership has consciously, although not always successfully, tried to institutionalize its informal politics. For instance, one attempt consisted of making public age limits for Party leaders. Deng Xiaoping and other Old Guard members continued to exercise their political influence after formal retirement from the Politburo in the late 1980s, thus creating a yawning gulf between nominal authority and informal power. In contrast, Jiang Zemin brought formal and informal power back into much closer alignment through institutionalization of informal politics. However, by retaining chairmanship of the Central Military Commission and sustaining a strong voice on critical and nonmilitary policy issues in the wake of the 16th Party Congress, Jiang has kept the gap between formal and informal power.

Rules and norms that are structuring the current leadership transition also shape China's political transition in a broader sense. Among many essential rules and principles, Chapter 2 examines the new ideological framework centered on the "Three Represents" and related institutional changes. In this chapter, Gang Lin points out that through the "Three Represents," the retiring Chinese leader Jiang Zemin intended to construct a new institutional foundation that would ultimately maintain his political dominance and continue his historical legacy. Lin argues that the advancement of the idea of "Three Represents" also demonstrates the Party's changing interests and its efforts to reconcile traditional doctrine with an increasingly diverse society. Such a theoretical innovation suggests that the Party has redefined itself as the vanguard for the entire Chinese population. By so doing, the

Party attempts to expand its power base and establish a holy alliance of political, economic, and intellectual elites. Lin also notes that the Party leadership has gradually adopted an open mind toward different "political civilizations" (*zhengzhi wenming*), realizing the necessity of coexistence and
mutual learning among various social systems and cultures in the world.

The growing diversification of the ruling Party as well as of Chinese society has presented a new challenge to the post-Jiang leadership in terms of
its ruling style and legitimacy. The new leadership apparently is seeking to
develop "intra-party democracy" through theoretical and institutional innovation without overhauling the existing one-party system. Indeed, the Party
officials, including the leading members of the Party think tank, the Central
Party School, have started to search for mechanisms to promote intra-party
democracy. They have even extolled the virtues of a so-called "Third
Way"—an institutional compromise between single-party authoritarianism
and multiparty democracy.[5] Principal measures under consideration are (1)
strengthening the function of Party committees at different levels through
serious implementation of collective leadership and majority rule; (2) em-
powering Party congresses to expand the base of power shared among the
Party elite; (3) developing check-and-balance mechanisms within the Party;
and (4) increasing intra-party electoral competition. According to Lin, Beijing's priority is to perpetuate the CCP's legitimacy through developing
intra-party democracy. However, it is uncertain whether the Party can reach
its goal without concomitantly opening the democratization process to the
entire society. Even if the new measures make the Party leadership more responsible to its members, they do not render it accountable to society as a
whole, Lin maintains. In the absence of meaningful restraints on the CCP's
monopoly of power and the consequent blurring of lines between Party and
state authority, China's political reform is likely to follow a gradualist trajectory with theoretical inconsistency and strategic ambiguity. Overall, the
Party's preemptive strategy of recruiting private entrepreneurs and developing intra-party democracy may serve to thwart social forces and public demand for radical political reform and multiparty democracy in the short
term. Given the Party's priorities and strategy regarding political reform in
the midst of incomplete property rights transformation and a not-so-inde-
pendent civil society in China, Lin concludes that the existing one-party
system is likely to continue to set parameters for China's institutional innovation for the foreseeable future.

Indeed, incomplete property rights transformation has yielded a mixed
economy in China that could help maintain the Party's rule. However, after

decades of gradual but sweeping transformation of China's property rights system, the fourth generation of Chinese leadership faces a fundamentally new relationship with the economy and society, and more importantly, with emerging pressure groups in China. As Xiaobo Hu argues in Chapter 3, the Chinese state delegated user rights to farmers and managers of state-owned enterprises while attempting to solve problems of low productivity and to increase output. In the late 1970s and early 1980s, the autonomy to make production decisions became the first step in fundamentally transforming China's socialist property rights structure. By creating a dual-track price system and promoting the development of the tertiary sector, the state incidentally formulated extractor rights and established an institutional arrangement favoring the exercise of informal extractor rights by bureaucrats and managers. Finally, when the state tried to minimize its financial burdens by merging companies and selling enterprises after 1997, it began—again incidentally—to complete the entire process of wholesale privatization and consolidation of some of the state assets into the hands of former bureaucrats and state-owned enterprise managers.

In other words, state policies during the reform era in China have mainly benefited insiders, that is, former government bureaucrats and state business managers. Indeed, state policies, aimed at solving specific sets of economic problems, have created a new institutional foundation for a post-Jiang state sector–private sector relationship. In this relationship, a triangle of insiders rules—current government officials and state business managers, former bureaucrats, and former state enterprise managers. By investigating both the recent history that has led to such institution building and the core elements of the state-private sector relationship, Xiaobo Hu finds inescapable consequences of past choices on current institutions. For the foreseeable future, the state-private sector relationship is likely to follow the old trajectory of unbalanced development along with political elitism. Unbalanced development will continue to benefit the insiders at the expense of workers and many others. Indeed, such a trend has been precisely reflected in the idea of "Three Represents" aggressively promoted by Jiang Zemin. This does not mean that all people in China have accepted the Chinese formula of property rights transformation, or "power privatization."[6] In addition to social protests from unemployed workers and underemployed farmers, as well as attacks from traditional ideologues and the New Left, some liberal intellectuals have also challenged such a model of uneven development, with great concern about social justice amid rapid economic transformation.[7]

To be sure, the transition to post-Jiang China is not only a political and economic transition, but also a transition for the entire society. In Chapter 4, Richard Madsen focuses on fundamental changes in relationships between the state and civil society. According to Madsen, the sweeping but unbalanced economic development of the last two decades or so has produced three different "worlds" or social systems in the country: "third-world China," "socialist China," and "newly industrializing China." Third-world China refers to inland central and western China, which is based on family-labor agriculture and maintained by informal, personal ties to kin and community and is outside effective control by the state. Such a social system is supported by Chinese traditional culture and specific institutional arrangements, such as the "household responsibility system" and "household registration system." Socialist China refers to the industrial northeast, which is still dominated by the legacy of state-owned enterprises, and in which social status depends on rank within bureaucratic hierarchies. Newly industrializing China refers to the coastal areas with their dynamic, export-oriented economic growth. Within this market-driven system, social status is based on money and individuals are loosely connected, but the boundary between state and civil society is blurring. The social order in newly industrializing China is maintained through authoritarian politics, which focuses on suppressing worker protests while allowing almost libertarian freedoms to owners and managers. Madsen argues that the three institutionally incompatible social systems are interconnected through corruption, migration, and personal networks, with most of resources flowing into newly industrializing China. The uneasy balance of the "three worlds" in China is inherently unstable. Further small changes in one area could lead to unpredictable, major, and perhaps disruptive, changes in another.

To hold this fragile unity of the three worlds together, the Communist Party has transformed itself into a corporatist party, Madsen argues. A corporatist party could lead the society through a "peaceful evolution" only by maintaining a reasonable degree of social stability and economic development for a long time while seeking to minimize the level of corruption and social protests. This might be a necessary, but not sufficient, condition for peaceful evolution. Madsen then points out the importance of formal institutions, such as formal procedures for nationwide democratic elections, in order to solve the contradictions among the three worlds in China. The only discernible hope is that the Chinese government has begun to develop such rules for free elections in the vast countryside. What would further challenge the power of the corporatist party is the growth of an independent middle class that does not have a stake in continuing corruption and can make use of the formal rules to pursue its interests in a peaceful manner. Finding institutionalized solutions (laws, regulations, welfare systems, and so on) to these pressing issues seems to be a high priority for the corporatist party. Whether the new generation of leaders will continue with the same energy remains to be seen.

At the same time that political, economic, and social transitions are taking place in China, major changes are occurring simultaneously in the international system and in China's foreign relations. The U.S. war on terrorism and China's entry into the World Trade Organization (WTO) have not only provided new opportunities for international cooperation, but also posed new strategic and economic challenges to China. As David Bachman observes in Chapter 5, Chinese leaders have been wondering about the shape, dimensions, norms, and rules of the post–September 11 international order. WTO accession will also increase China's exposure to international market trends and regulations. Whereas China's rapidly growing stake in the international system limits the government's freedom of action, the constraints are not so tight as to prevent Chinese leaders from having some freedom of choice within existing international institutions, norms, and practices.

Throughout the past several years, according to Bachman, three central agencies have been influential over China's foreign policy: the People's Liberation Army, the Ministry of Foreign Affairs, and the Ministry of Foreign Trade and Economic Cooperation. While each agency has particular stakes in China's open-door policy, it always seeks opportunities to maximize its advantage, especially when the leadership is divided and focused on power struggles.

The politics of elite succession will undoubtedly color Chinese foreign policymaking. Significant changes had been under way some time before the 16th Party Congress. However, until power is consolidated by the fourth generation of leaders, continuity is likely to be the hallmark of the new leadership. While Hu Jintao enjoys photo opportunities and much publicity, management of international affairs will probably actually become increasingly subject to bureaucratic influence. Foreign policy decisions will become fairly routine and predictable. Nevertheless, Bachman cautions that should Jiang continue to maintain his influence, a more disjointed style of policymaking might prevail, as the institutions of decision making would become loci for the struggle for power. Even so, to the extent that exogenous developments are limited, it is unlikely that there will be broad departures in foreign policy, because foreign policy has not been a critical issue in China's succession politics historically.

Indeed, in the absence of a clear-cut power transfer from third- to fourth-generation leaders or a game in which the "winner takes all" among different political factions within the Party, outsiders should not expect abrupt policy reorientation in China's domestic and foreign policies during the period of leadership transition. Still, fundamental political changes will take place in the long term, with the foundations constructed during this leadership transition. This volume provides a general analysis of Chinese politics in transition to the post-Jiang era by exploring such institutional foundations as the new ideology and the new political rules that have been emerging and will likely dominate China in the near future, the rising political significance of the mixed economy, the ever-changing relationship between the state and civil society, and the new sources of Chinese foreign policy.

Short of political transparency in China, speculation is, to some extent, unavoidable. Studies of political behavior could be enhanced, however, by thoroughly examining the institutional foundations that have been undergoing gradual transformation through two decades of economic, social, and political reform in China. Contributors to this volume de-emphasize the possibility of a swift political or policy change immediately following the 16th Party Congress. Instead, they examine gradual but profound shifts in China's politics, economy, and society during the entire process of political succession. Such shifts are preparing a likely significant departure in Chinese politics under the fourth generation leadership. With such a theoretical focus, this volume attempts to offer a better understanding of China's ongoing transition as well as the implications of that transition for the world.

Notes

The editors would like to gratefully acknowledge the encouragement and support of this book project from Joseph F. Brinley of the Woodrow Wilson Center Press, the Center's Asia Program, and the Department of Political Science at Clemson University. We also want to express our deep gratitude to Lowell Dittmer, Richard Madsen, and David Bachman for their valuable contributions and for their patience and cooperation during the editorial process. Many thanks also go to the useful comments from the anonymous reviewers of an earlier draft of the entire book manuscript, the constructive suggestions by Dorothy Solinger, Martin Slann, and Amy McCreedy to an earlier draft of this introduction, and the able editorial assistance of Yamile Kahn. Views expressed in this book are of the authors only.

1. The CCP convened eight national congresses between 1949 and 1997, but the Party-state's supreme power was not transferred from one leader to another at any of

these congresses. China's first paramount leader Mao Zedong served as Party chairman until he died in 1976. His designated successor Hua Guofeng assumed the chairmanship before the Party's 11th Congress in 1977. Deng Xiaoping served as China's de facto paramount leader between 1978 and 1994. During this period, Hu Yaobang took the Party chairmanship from Hua Guofeng prior to the Party's 12th Congress (1982); Zhao Ziyang succeeded Hu Yanbang before the 13th Party Congress (1987); and Jiang Zemin assumed the Party leadership three years before the Party's 14th Congress (1992). While the Party has regularly convened its national congresses every five years since 1977, internal power succession was far from being formalized before the 16th Congress.

2. Literally, the "Three Represents" means that the Party should represent the developmental requirements of China's advanced productive forces, the developing orientation of China's advanced culture, and the fundamental interests of the overwhelming majority of the Chinese people. Ideologically, the essence of this term is to redefine the Party as an ever-innovating organization corresponding to China's socioeconomic and cultural development and allowing private entrepreneurs to join the Party.

3. Douglass C. North, *Institutions, Institutional Change, and Economic Performance* (Cambridge; N.Y.: Cambridge University Press, 1990).

4. For example, see John Pomfret, "Chinese Leader Throws a Curve: Jiang's Reluctance to Retire Could Spark Power Struggle," *Washington Post*, July 21, 2002, p. A1; Susan V. Lawrence, "The New Leadership: It Ain't Over, Till It's Over," *Far Eastern Economic Review*, August 8, 2002, pp. 24–25; Susan V. Lawrence, "Jiang Finds It Hard to Let Go," *Far Eastern Economic Review*, September 12, 2002, pp. 34–36; Erik Eckholm, "China's Leader Won't Hold On, Anonymous Author Says," *The New York Times*, September 5, 2002; Erik Eckholm, "Time for the Changing of China's Aging Guard—or Not," *The New York Times*, September 22, 2002; Jeremy Page, "Noises Off as China Sets Stage for Succession," *Reuters News*, September 12, 2002; Erik Eckholm, "China's New Leader Promises Not to Sever Tether to Jiang," *The New York Times*, November 21, 2002.

5. Jeremy Page, "China Opens Up Political Debate to Strengthen Party," *Reuters News*, July 20, 2002.

6. Xiaobo Hu, "Transition of Property Rights in China: The Institutional Origins," Entrepreneurial Leadership Working Paper Series 02-101 (The Arthur M. Spiro Center for Entrepreneurial Leadership, Clemson University, Clemson, S.C., 2002); He Qinglian, "Comprehensive Analysis of Current Social Structural Changes in China," *Shuwu*, no. 3 (2000).

7. Qin Hui, "Ershi Shiji Mo Zhongguo de Jingji Zhuangui, Shehui Gongzheng yu Minzhuhua Wenti" [Issues on China's Economic Transformation, Social Justice and Democratization at the End of the 20th Century], in *Zhuanxingzhong de Zhongguo Zhengzhi Yu Zhengzhixue Fazhan* [Political Science and China in Transition] (Beijing: Renmin University of China, July 2002).

Chapter 1

Chinese Leadership Succession to the Fourth Generation

Lowell Dittmer

Leadership succession is unusually important in Chinese politics for two reasons: first, because power is highly concentrated at the top, so that whoever ultimately succeeds can make a great deal of difference to the political system; and second, because the transfer of power is relatively open-ended. Both of these features are less true than in the past. There has been considerable decentralization and devolution of power since the death of Mao, diminishing the relative power of the center. Moreover, while decentralization and a carefully limited democratization may have broadened the range of possible policy outcomes at regional and local levels, the technocratization of the elite seems to have narrowed the range of plausible outcomes at the center since the end of the Mao era, when the leadership could quite conceivably have fallen into the hands of a clique committed to the radical transformation of Chinese domestic and foreign policy. Still, the central Chinese Communist Party (CCP) leadership remains essentially monocratic and continues to exert virtually boundless power, and although differences among potential successors are subtle and publicly minimized, there is still considerable uncertainty. Even during the several months before the most recent 16th National Congress of the CCP, for example, how much power would be ceded at the top and exactly who would succeed to it remained far from certain.

What is distinctive and what is generic about the Chinese Communist leadership succession scenario? All hierarchical leadership regimes must undergo succession amid a modicum of uncertainty, experienced either postmortem or premortem (i.e., after or before the death of the incumbent leader), but the range of uncertainty and the impact of the choice are greater in authoritarian dictatorships, where succession procedures typically remain relatively uninstitutionalized and immune from oversight or critical feedback. China is attempting to make the transition to a more institutionalized succession procedure for the sake of greater stability and predictability. Yet this transition has proved difficult, in part because of the ambiguity of the goal: If the purpose of more stable succession arrangements is to minimize uncertainty, would not the most stable succession be no change at all? After all, who really knows what succession will bring when the heir apparent avoids jeopardizing his chances by never expressing an original idea? Moreover, the "principle" of "stability above all" (*wending yadao yiqie*) is subject to varying practical interpretations. In addition to principles, interests are also very much at stake, both ideal (as in policy "lines") and material. While the coalition of young reformers and miscellaneous anti-Jiang elements place their faith in an abstract, generalizable norm, Jiang's supporters fear among other things that transition to a generation unimplicated in the 1989 crackdown might lead to a move to "rehabilitate" (*pingfan*) the protesters, endangering the interests of those implicated and precipitating uncontainable controversy. Thus, in a transition Chinese succession arrangements are analogous to the mixed-genre status of the political-economic system as a whole.

Two features are more specific to the Chinese case of succession than other hierarchical regimes. First, China is unusual in the amount of anticipatory attention devoted to this particular rite of passage. Throughout CCP history, succession has been a source of inordinate concern and occasional outbursts of concentrated, disruptive strife. Indeed, it can be argued that most if not all of the "line struggles" that have roiled CCP politics over the years have turned around the issue of succession. This is so even though the Party-state has completed only two full-fledged successions since 1949 (i.e., from Mao to Hua Guofeng in 1976, and from Deng to Jiang Zemin in 1989), amid rather more numerous elite cleavages and purges. The reason that struggles within the elite outnumber completed successions relates to a second feature peculiar to the Chinese case: the marked preference for premortem succession arrangements. Owing perhaps to a political tradition of dynastic succession in the absence of primogeniture, the Chinese leadership has invested a great deal of political capital in the preliminary making and recurrent reconsideration of anticipatory succession arrangements. Thus, the Gao–Rao split in the mid-1950s emerged in the context of Mao's express desire to retreat to a less active role and put others on the "first front," and the decade-long Cultural Revolution involved the rotation of first Liu Shaoqi, then Lin Biao, then (more tentatively) Wang Hongwen, and finally Hua Guofeng, into the precarious role of heir apparent. Notwithstanding Deng Xiaoping's avowed determination to institutionalize the process, he himself made two abortive selections (i.e., Hu Yaobang and Zhao Ziyang) before finally settling on Jiang Zemin. In contrast to the People's Republic of China (PRC), many structurally analogous socialist republics were resigned to postmortem deferment of the issue (e.g., Khrushchev's succession to Stalin, Brezhnev's to Khrushchev, and Honecker's to Ulbricht).

The history of the CCP succession issue may be divided into three eras: the pre-Mao era, the Maoist succession, and the post-Mao era. During the pre-Mao era, succession crises were nasty, brutish, and short. Succession was premortem and invariably involuntary, consisting of a confrontation between a discredited incumbent and the rest of the Politburo, who would ultimately force him out, often with the backstage help of the Comintern. Yet they were mercifully brief, an ambush sprung by would-be successors, which was not planned or manipulated by the incumbent. The decisive difference of Mao's era had to do with the charismatic personality of the incumbent, which derived from the improbable success of his record. Against all odds (and with a dollop of luck), the Chinese Communist revolution under Mao's direction succeeded in defeating and banishing the ruling Nationalist regime and in establishing uncontested sovereignty over a unified mainland for the first time since the fall of the Qing. Mao's batting average after Liberation was more mixed, particularly during his last two decades, but his regime can plausibly claim to have transformed the Chinese political spectrum in a lasting way and to have established China as a world power. Yet ironically, the Maoist succession scenario was the worst in CCP history, consisting of incessant premortem intrigue, coup plots, and power struggles, only to culminate in a postmortem succession crisis in which Mao's default successor proved too weak to survive. For the first

time in CCP history, the incumbent intervened repeatedly in premortem
succession arrangements, as a way of motivating/manipulating and balancing off would-be rivals. It was in the shadow of this nightmare that the
Deng Xiaoping regime introduced sweeping reforms, attempting not only
to arrange for the premortem succession of the top leader but to institutionalize the orderly replacement of an entire generation of veteran incumbents.[1] At the provincial and local levels, the introduction of term limits
and retirement packages has on whole been quite successful.[2] At the top,
the picture has been more ambiguous: Deng Xiaoping arranged for his retirement from formal positions of authority but then made a mockery of his
own arrangements by intervening informally to replace his own successor
designates. Yet he did finally succeed in stage-managing the CCP's first
orderly premortem succession, ceding all formal power in 1989 and relinquishing informal influence (at the brink of death) in late 1994.

The most recent PRC succession arrangements have proceeded in two
distinct arenas. One is the formal political arena, where the selection of
delegates for the 16th Congress, held November 8–14, 2002, after a myste-
rious two-month delay, was conducted with considerable transparency
from bottom to top (in accord with top-down prescriptions). The second is
the informal elite arena, where retiring incumbents and prospective successors maneuvered, typically with elaborate subtlety and political opacity, to
rearrange intersecting career tracks. Both of these contests took place
within a vast political structure that is essentially hierarchical but in fact in-
volves vast functional duplication along multiple tracks at the formal level,
plus myriad informal short circuits. Some positions are still inherently better than others, which accounts for the intense level of competition during
succession periods. The structure might be compared semi-facetiously to a
game of chutes and ladders: Positions that lead upward are "ladders,"
while those that lead downward to quiet political oblivion (if no longer,
usually, to public disgrace) are "chutes." The ladder positions, consisting
essentially of "line" executive posts in the Party, government, and army,
have the power to make and execute decisions, and lead upward to still
greater power. The chutes are showcase sinecures in the legislative arenas
scattered throughout the Party-state, notably the National People's Congress (NPC), the Chinese People's Political Consultative Conference
(CPPCC), the non-CCP "democratic parties" (*minzhu dangpai*), the procu-
ratorial/legal system, and the auxiliary organizations that possess the ap-
pearance of power without its substance. Those in ladder positions, looking forward to bright political futures, tend to comport themselves

obsequiously; while those on the way out, with less at stake, may opt to play the righteous official (*qingguan*) in defense of high principle. Of course, this is an oversimplification of a complex reality in which there are infinite gradations and compromises between having power and not having it, where the seemingly "good" positions may not be fully exploited for tactical or diplomatic reasons while seemingly inferior positions may become politically consequential because of the personal status of the role occupant. Peng Zhen, Wan Li, and Qiao Shi, for example, the last three chairmen of the NPC Standing Committee, have expanded this hitherto "flower pot" role by taking more "principled" stands. Although traditionally scorned as "rubber stamps," China's legislative forums, under the leadership of illustrious cadres consigned to chutes before their time, have thus expanded their authority considerably in the past two decades.[3] Even that institutional relic of the united front, the CPPCC, assumed greater prominence under the leadership of Jiang Zemin's old rival Li Ruihuan, after the latter was forced to relinquish his Politburo portfolio as leader of the Party's propaganda work.

The Formal Process

Let us begin by looking at progress in the arena that is easiest to examine, the bottom-up formal selection of delegates. Preparations began at the 6th Plenum of the 15th CCP Central Committee held in September 2001. The Party stipulated that the election of the 2,120 delegates to attend the 16th Congress, representing some 66 million CCP members, would be the top priority work in 2002, to be conducted in conjunction with "work style transformation" and "investigation and study" of major theoretical and practical problems. Delegates were elected (by secret ballot, and with multiple candidacies, or *cha'e xuanju*, although the "margin of elimination," or *cha'e*, was only 12.5 percent, no more than in 1997) in 38 electoral units, including the 31 provincial units, the central organizations (*zhongyang jiguan*), and the People's Liberation Army (PLA). Delegate selection was completed by the end of February 2002, with the election results being reported to the 16th Congress Delegates Credentials Investigation Committee for approval. (Special guests to the Congress were also invited, at the discretion of the central authorities.) Of the 2,120 delegates thus selected, 97.5 percent had joined the CCP after Liberation in 1949, and 31.9 percent joined after the Third Plenum of the 11th Congress in December 1978; 63.1 percent of the delegates were 55 years of age or less;

and average age of delegates was 52.5 years, about eight months less than
the average age of delegates to the 15th Congress. Regarding education,
some 91.7 percent of the delegates had four-year college degrees or gradu-
ate degrees, many of these from China's leading schools, compared to 70.7
percent in 1992.[4] Some 18 percent of the delegates were female, 10.8 percent were ethnic minorities, and an overwhelming majority (75.7 percent)
were Party or government officials. Reformers in the Party lobbied for a
larger margin of elimination when Congress delegates (s)elected Central
Committee (CC) members, and for some margin when the latter elected
members of the Politburo. Although this indicated a rising tide of interest
in "intra-party democracy," neither request succeeded, as other political
reforms (e.g., the 1998 suggestion that village-level elections be gradually
and incrementally expanded to the level of townships/counties) have also
languished since the 15th Party Congress.[5] Instead, the Jiang leadership
agreed to introduce "elite democracy," that is, inducting "trustworthy experts" from a broader cross-section of society into the top echelons, recruiting officials into the mid-ranking bureaucratic levels through "public
exams," and other such modest adjustments.

Delegate selection presupposed the reorganization of the province-level
Party committees, which the central leadership proceeded to undertake.
The emphasis was on four features: increasing interprovince personnel rotation, rejuvenation of leading cadres, higher education credentials, and orderly procedure. By March 2002, sixty-two leading Party and government
positions in eleven of China's thirty-one provinces, autonomous regions,
and centrally administered municipalities had been "adjusted." That includes the adjustment of Party secretaries in five provinces (Jiangxi,
Hubei, Hainan, Yunnan, and Qinghai) and one autonomous region (Inner
Mongolia), and of governors in four provinces (Jiangxi, Shandong, Hunan,
and Yunnan) and one municipality (Shanghai). By June 2002, seventeen of
the provinces, as well as some twenty ministries and commissions, had
completed turnover and reelection of their Party committees, with more
personnel movements occurring in the rest of the regions during the run-up
to the Congress. Likewise, around 200 mid-level and senior PLA posts at
both central headquarters units and the regional commands have changed
hands. These shifts are significant not only because the new regional leaders would then supervise the election of the 2,120 delegates and special
guests who would attend the Congress, but because the new Party secretaries, governors, mayors, and PLA officers/commissars themselves might
then be elected to the ruling CC.[6] Of the new crop of sixty-two Party secre-

taries and governors (for China's thirty-one provinces, municipalities, and ethnic autonomous regions), more than 82 percent were college educated, up from less than 54 percent in 1987. But nearly all were educated in Chinese universities—only one of China's new provincial leaders, Zhang Dejiang, party secretary of Zhejiang Province (and new Politburo member), was educated abroad, having received his B.A. from Kim Il Song Comprehensive University in North Korea.

More than half of the members and candidates of the incumbent CC were retired because of age, a turnover rate roughly corresponding to that in the 15th Congress. Among the 198 full CC members, 112 (56 percent) are new, compared to 59 percent of new members in 1997. In accord with the new age restrictions, all CC members born in or before 1937 (i.e., age 65 years or above) retired (including Hua Guofeng, and Li Tieying, who was born in 1936). Exceptions were Luo Gan (who was promoted to the Politburo Standing Committee); Ismail Amat, Cao Gangchuan (elected to the Politburo and the Central Military Commission); Li Guixian; and Xu Kuangdi. The average age of the 356 full and alternate CC members is 55.4 years, and more than a fifth of these are under age 50. Of the full members for whom we have reliable data (86 percent), 44.4 percent are in the 60-to-69 age cohort, while the other 41.9 percent are below age 60 (of whom a mere 3.5 percent are less than 50). Of the 356 full and alternate members, 35 (9.8 percent) are members of national minorities, of whom 15 (7.5 percent) are full CC members, which is about the same number as in the 15th CC (14). In terms of educational credentials, fully 82.4 percent of the 198 full members had completed college; 17.2 percent of this group also had postgraduate degrees (30 M.A.'s and 4 Ph.D.'s), and 16 percent are trained engineers. About a third (31.8 percent) of the 198 hail from regional geographic bases, while 30.3 percent belong to government ministries, 16.2 percent are from the Party apparatus, and 20.7 percent from the PLA. Thus, an overwhelming majority of the full CC members are full-time public officials (two, or 1 percent, are CEOs of state-owned enterprises, and one alternate is an entrepreneur).[7]

The CC Organization Department held a meeting in June 2001 to discuss stepping up efforts to promote female cadre visibility for the 16th Congress, and the preparatory group for the Congress accordingly proposed to elect two women to the Politburo: Wu Yi, age 63 (former minister of foreign trade, alternate Politburo member, and a Zhu Rongji protégé), and Chen Zhili (minister of education). Only the nomination of "iron lady" Wu Yi was successful; she was also slated to become a vice premier in charge of foreign relations and relations with international nongovernmental organizations. Chen Zhili was elected a full member of the CC, but was reportedly slated to become state councilor in charge of culture and education. In addition, ten ministry-level female officials were elected full or alternate CC members, including Wu Aiying, deputy secretary of the Shandong Province Party committee, Sun Chunlan, deputy secretary of the Liaoning Province Party committee, and Meng Xiaosi, vice minister of culture, were elected members or alternate members of the CC. A few entrepreneurs were included among the 2,120 delegates to the 16th Congress, but none made it to full CC membership; Zhang Ruimin (chief executive officer of the Haier corporation in Shandong Province) was elected as an alternate. Altogether, 27 (about 7 percent) of the 356 full and alternate members of the CC are female, although only 5 (2.5 percent) are full members (down from 7 in the 15th CC).

China's PLA (comprising 1.8 million troops)—the power that comes from the barrel of a gun (but must be commanded by the Party)—was represented at the Party congress by a sizable delegation, in preparation for which the PLA leadership was reorganized along guidelines emphasizing professionalization and rejuvenation. Senior cadres tend to believe that one way of bringing in new people while minimizing the risk of disloyalty is to promote children of high-level cadres. The so-called princeling party (*taizidang*) has prospered recently in the armed forces, and no less than in the Party. Thus, Zhang Xiang, son of former Defense Minister General Zhang Aiping, was made deputy commander of the (missile unit) Second Artillery Corps (in July 2001 he was also promoted from major general to lieutenant general); and Peng Xiaofeng, son of General Peng Xuefeng (a famous general during the War of Resistance against Japan), has been promoted to deputy political commissar of the Lanzhou Military Region. Other scions of legendary military figures slated for promotion include Lieutenant General Su Rongsheng (son of General Su Yu), to deputy commander of the Beijing Military Region; Lieutenant General Luo Dongjin (son of Marshal Luo Ronghuan), deputy political commissar of the Second Artillery Corps; Lieutenant General Liu Yuan (son of Liu Shaoqi), deputy political commissar of the Armed Police Force; and Lieutenant General Tan Dongsheng (son of former State Council Vice Premier Tan Zhenlin), deputy commander of the Guangzhou Military Region.[8] But the upward mobility of children of high-level cadres, however demonstrative of the increasing importance of inherited privilege in this post-revolutionary system, has thus far been relegated to deputy positions several steps from the central leadership. This pattern is even more transparent in the civilian political apparatus. Moreover, in terms of policy, the "princelings" cannot be said to constitute a "faction" or even a shared policy perspective, except perhaps for a vague vested interest in the political status quo.

The central leadership of the PLA is of course concentrated in the Central Military Commission (CMC). The CMC elected by the CC of the 15th Congress at its first plenum directly after the Congress consisted of seven members, led by Chairman Jiang Zemin; Hu Jintao was promoted to the CMC (as vice chairman) in 1999. After keeping China (and the rest of the world) on tenterhooks throughout much of the year about whether he would retire from his leadership of the CMC, Jiang decided in the end not to do so, although some continued to speculate that he would stay on only until the 10th NPC in March 2003, when he would step down from this post along with the term-limited retirement from his position as chief of state. This was wishful thinking, and indeed the latest reports from Beijing indicate that Jiang intends to stay on for at least two or three years, to chair a body otherwise sorely lacking political figures with any military experience. Jiang has relied on the precedent of Deng Xiaoping, who retained the CMC chairmanship while yielding all other posts from the 13th Congress in 1987 until the fall of 1989, enabling him to commandeer the suppression of the Tiananmen protests without even holding a seat on the Politburo. The results of the 16th Congress were that while Jiang stayed on as chairman, age limits applied to everyone else, eliminating former CMC vice chairmen Chi Haotian and Zhang Wannian, as well as Yu Yongbo, director of the General Political Department, and Fu Quanyou, chief of general staff. General Cao Gangchuan, director of the General Armament Department, moved into a second vice chairmanship, also gaining a seat on the Politburo (and became defense minister at the 10th NPC). General Cao, a protégé of Deng Xiaoping who previously served under Deng's son-in-law General He Ping, worked closely with Hu Jintao in 1999, when the latter was in charge of getting the army out of business, closing thousands of PLA enterprises (to the indignation of a number of generals). General Guo Boxiong, 59, became third vice chairman; Guo had entered the CMC from the PLA Lanzhou Military Region at the same time that Hu was appointed ranking vice chair at the 4th Plenum of the 15th CC in September 1999. This troika of Hu, Cao, and Guo thus might comprise the nucleus of a fourth-generation PLA leadership. Other CMC members include Xu Caihou, 58, director of the General Political Department, who entered the CMC with Guo Boxiong; Liang Guanglie, former commander the Nanjing Military Region, who became the new chief of general staff; Liao Xilong, Sino-Vietnamese war hero, who was appointed director of the General Logistics Department; and Li Jinai, former commissar of the General Armaments Department, who became its director.[9] One of the explanations given for Jiang's decision to stay on after relinquishing his CC membership the day before was to monitor Taiwan policy, which Jiang feared might otherwise veer out of control under the hawkish leadership of Guo Boxiong, Cao Gangchuan, and Liang Guanglie.[10]

The organizational nuts and bolts of this sweeping "adjustment" were controlled by Jiang Zemin via Zeng Qinghong, Jiang's deputy secretary in Shanghai whom he brought with him to head the Central Organization Department as well as his own office. This naturally aroused suspicion that Jiang was using personnel policy to tilt the factional balance in favor of his own followers—a suspicion presumably contributing to Zeng's failure to be elected to the Politburo in three attempts preceding the 16th Party Congress (where he finally gained that promotion, ranking fifth, as well as the ranking position on the CC Secretariat). Statistically, it is demonstrable that Jiang's clients fare better than average—although Jiang's imprimatur was hardly a guarantee for unfettered upward mobility, as Zeng's own experience illustrates. Huang Ju, promoted to the sixth-ranking position on the Politburo Standing Committee and slated to be deputy vice premier, is a charter member of the "Shanghai gang," having served on the Shanghai Municipality Party Committee from 1983 to 1991 (the first six years as Jiang's deputy Party secretary), before succeeding Zhu Rongji as Shanghai mayor in 1991, and becoming a member the Politburo and the secretariat in 1994. Jia Qinglin, Beijing Party secretary and a longtime Jiang associate, was so damaged by the exposure of a multibillion-yuan smuggling and corruption scandal in Xiamen in 1999–2000 (previously he was Party secretary and his wife was director of foreign trade in Fujian Province) that he was expected to be pushed into semi-retirement as a NPC or CPPCC vice chairman. On May 22, 2002, Jia Qinglin was unexpectedly reelected Beijing Party secretary, keeping him in the Politburo, and at the 16th Congress he was promoted to the Politburo Standing Committee and slated as chair of the CPPCC. Liu Qi, who played a key role in Beijing's successful bid for the 2008 Olympics as Beijing's mayor, was promoted to the Politburo. Guangdong Party Secretary Li Changchun, another Jiang protégé, was promoted to the Politburo in 1997 and took the Guangdong Party secretaryship in the next year after spending nearly a decade in Henan Province (as vice governor, governor, and party secretary). Wu Bangguo, who worked as deputy secretary (1985 to 1991) and secretary (1991 to 1994) of the Shanghai Municipal Party Committee, before being promoted to the Politburo (1992) and to a vice premiership on the State Council (1994), was promoted to the Politburo Standing Committee and is slated to chair the NPC Standing Committee in March 2003.

Although Politburo appointments seem to have remained under the control of Jiang's machine, the perceived organizational interests of Hu Jintao have not been completely ignored. The CC Organization Department stipulated that a number of outstanding cadres in their thirties, with experience at the grassroots level, should be selected as deputy leaders at province and ministry levels, and that other relatively young and promising cadres be selected from existing province-level leadership groups, ministries, and national-level commissions for further study abroad.[11] As former first secretary of the Communist Youth League (CYL), the emphasis on rejuvenation played to Hu's advantage. When the Politburo Standing Committee signaled its interest in adding one or two young people to the Politburo and the CC Secretariat, a number of Hu's associates were considered, including, among others, Zhou Qiang, 41, first secretary of the Central Committee of the CYL; Li Keqiang, 46, governor of Henan Province and Zhou's predecessor at the CYL; Zhao Leji, 44, governor of Qinghai Province; Xi Jinping, 48, governor of Fujian Province (and son of Party veteran Xi Zhongxun); Quan Zhezhu, alternate member of the 15th CC and executive vice governor of Jilin Province; and Wu Aiying, alternate member of the 15th CC and deputy secretary of the Party committee for Shandong Province. In addition to Zhou Quang and Li Keqiang, Liu Peng, executive deputy head of the Central Propaganda Department, and Zhao Shi, deputy director of the State Administration of Radio, Film and Television, were both CYL secretaries. Whereas Li, Liu, and Zhao all worked under Hu when he was CYL first secretary, Zhou Qiang was personally picked by Hu to chair the CYL Central Committee in Hu's capacity of Politburo Standing Committee member. Other members of the CYL group who used to work with Hu include Fujian Provincial Party Secretary Song Defu and Minister of Justice Zhang Fusen.[12] Of these presumptive Hu supporters, Zhou Qiang, Li Keqiang, Zhao Leji, Xi Jinping, Song Defu, and Zhang Fusen all were elected full members of the CC, and Quan Zhezhu became an alternate member. In addition to the CYL, the growing "Tsinghua gang," the largest "old school tie" group in the elite, should, ceteris paribus, have an elective affinity for fellow alumnus Hu Jintao (although in some cases, such as Zhu Rongji, Wu Bangguo, and Huang Ju, their loyalties might be trumped by membership on other lists, in this case, the "Shanghai gang").[13] And as we have indicated, the reorganization of the CMC did not redound to Hu's disadvantage, although the chairmanship was withheld.

While factional vested interests are not hard to detect in this new lineup, an extensive transformation of China's leadership must nonetheless be conceded, perhaps the most sweeping since reform was initiated 25 years ago. More than half of the CC members and alternate members were phased out in accord with age limitations, 14 of the 24 full Politburo members are new faces and all but one (Hu Jintao) of the nine Politburo Standing Committee members made room for younger blood. Also striking is the increasing decentralization of the leadership, with a third of the CC membership hailing from provincial bases, 50 percent of the Politburo, and 44 percent of the Standing Committee.[14] The CC Secretariat, now led by Zeng Qinghong, has had a sweeping turnover: New members include Liu Yunshan (head of the Propaganda Department); Zhou Yongkang (former Sichuan Party secretary); He Guoqiang (replacing Zeng as head of the Organization Department); Wang Gang (in charge of the CC General Office); General Xu Caihou (political work in the PLA); and He Yong (Party discipline). Other new appointments worth watching are Hui Liangyu, the only national minority member in the Politburo, who became vice premier in charge of agriculture; Zeng Peiyan, Politburo member and minister of the State Development and Planning Commission, became vice premier in charge of trade; and Zeng Qinghong's pal Zhou Yongkang, former Sichuan Party secretary and now a member of the Secretariat, who also got a seat in the State Council to assume responsibility for public security affairs. Although Jiang's apparent strategy in monopolizing the personnel appointment process was to block Hu from consolidating his own power base by preempting all available vacancies, it is hard to predict what will happen with so many new people improvising to meet the challenges of high unemployment, growing economic inequality and corruption, a looming banking crisis, the economic difficulties that will inevitably accompany World Trade Organization compliance, and growing pressure for real political reform.

Informal Politics

In the PRC, political informality tends—with certain important exceptions—to correlate directly with formal power; that is, the more formal power one has, the more informal power. This is because decision-making discretion gives one the necessary latitude to override the rules, and decision-making discretion tends to be greatest at the top of the hierarchy. After nearly three decades under the charismatic leadership of Mao Zedong, the surviving Chinese leadership decided to shift from a transformational leadership style, which launched one "revolutionary" breakthrough after another, sometimes with economically catastrophic results, to a transactional style of leadership that would preside over a more disjointed incremental style of change.[15] Such incremental change reflected a clear path dependency, which meant that the leadership would yield part of its range of discretion in policy choices to historical precedent. This entailed imposing a framework of rules on the leadership and curtailing its informal power, which has been exploited in the new market environment for personal corruption. Curtailment of informal power has been implemented via the strictly timed schedule of leadership meetings at all levels; the introduction of the rule of law to which the Party leadership, initially exempt, is increasingly expected to comply; and the introduction of term and age limit rules. Beginning at the bottom, which has always been under greatest constraint, and moving cautiously upward, over the past two decades the rules of the game for the CCP leadership have been institutionalized; the area of widest leadership discretion remained at the top, especially during successions. Yet the new rules of the game were gaining currency even here, reducing the latitude of the heir apparent or that of his conceivable rivals to undertake transformational initiatives or indeed to deviate more than marginally from an increasingly lock-step collective leadership consensus. The engineering background of the new elite (e.g., nine out of nine on the new Politburo Standing Committee are engineers) provided excellent socialization for this patient, "technocratic" role definition. By the time of the 16th Congress, the locus of the resistance to further leadership institutionalization had been reduced to the problem of the paramount leader, as everyone else in the Politburo Standing Committee publicly signaled an intention to retire in accord with the new rules. Yet as Jiang saw it, he still had three options: complete retirement (*quan tui*), vacating all three of his leadership posts; quasi-retirement (*ban tui*), stepping down from his leadership of the Party and State but remaining CMC chairman; and *bu tui*, or retention of the position of Party General Secretary as well, which he sometimes insisted was not age or term limited. The evolution of the leadership consensus on this issue, and of Jiang's rationale for deviating from that consensus, is worth following in somewhat more detail.

The preliminary list of slated members of the CC's leadership organs for the 16th National Congress was drawn up in the summer 2001 meetings at Beidaihe, anticipating that Jiang Zemin, then 75, would give up all three of the executive positions he held from 1989 to 2002—president of the state, general secretary of the CCP, and chairman of the CMC—and retire from the Politburo in favor of Hu Jintao. Hu's portfolio of Party affairs, as well as his positions as president of the Central Party School and vice president of the state, would be assumed by Zeng Qinghong, who finally got a seat on the Politburo Standing Committee. Premier Li Peng would retire after five years as chairman of the NPC upon convention of that body in the spring of 2003. Though Li Peng heads a powerful faction in government, he is deeply unpopular in China for the role he played in the decision to crack down at Tiananmen (Li is the last member of the leadership directly implicated in that decision), and he and his family are tainted by incessant rumors of corruption. Premier Zhu Rongji would also retire from all posts (including even his contemplated deanship of the school of business administration at Tsinghua), to be succeeded by Vice Premier Wen Jiabao, Zhu's choice to succeed him. The new lineup of the Politburo Standing Committee would thus include Hu Jintao as convener, Wen Jiabao, and Zeng Qinghong in the three leading positions, followed possibly by Wu Bangguo, Li Changchun, and Li Peng protégé, Luo Gan. At this time Li Ruihuan, who would only be 68 at the time of the Congress, was still considered likely to remain on the Standing Committee, moving up from the CPPCC to chairmanship of the NPC. This arrangement, retaining roughly the same factional balance by permitting retiring members to select their own successors, was considered consistent with the spirit of generational succession.

The initial understanding that Jiang should retire completely after one more term was first articulated in the preparatory meeting for the 15th Congress in 1997, when it was agreed (in what is now characterized as an informal understanding without binding power) that 70 should be the cut-off age for further service on the Politburo. While the immediate incentive was to provide a pretext for eliminating Jiang's rival, NPC Chairman Qiao Shi and former vice chairman of the Party Central Advisor Commission Bo Yibo recommended that Jiang, as "core," should be an exception to the rule. This was to be a one-shot deal based on the premise that Jiang would step down at the end of his term, as Qiao has subsequently made clear.[16] Jiang's acceptance of the senior veterans' counsel was selective, however, welcoming Qiao's retirement from the NPC but dropping the idea that Qiao then be rotated into the position of state president (to avoid, it was argued, Party–state overlap should Jiang take both posts), preferring to keep that position himself. Jiang's chief concern at that time seemed to be consolidating his hold on the three leading positions in the Party, state, and PLA. In summer 1999, prior to the annual Beidaihe retreat, he emulated Deng's prior tactic of soliciting support from retired veterans; for example, Liu Huaqing (vice chair of the CMC, former Politburo Standing Committee member) and Song Ping (former Politburo Standing Committee member) praised Jiang as Deng's choice to lead the Party from the 14th to the 16th Congress, lauding his effectiveness in uncertain times.[17] Nor did Jiang neglect to cultivate his ideological base on the left, as Deng Liqun favorably contrasted Jiang with Deng Xiaoping, who he said was too preoccupied with economics to bring ideology and politics to the fore as Jiang had done with his "Three Emphases" (see below).[18] In November 1999, Li Peng, Hu Jintao, Liu Huaqing, Song Ping, Zhang Wannian (CMC vice chairman), Ding Guangen (member of the Politburo and the CC Secretariat), and others all voiced support for Jiang's continuing leadership.[19] Upon the abrupt resignation of Boris Yeltsin in January 2000, Jiang immediately requisitioned a raft of recent books analyzing the fall of the Soviet Union, which ostensibly moved him to reflect about his place in history and the need to protect his legacy. Thus, in early 2000 the Politburo announced that Ding Guangen would chair a committee to draft the "Ten Great Achievements of the Third Generation of Leaders with Jiang Zemin at the Core," but this effort ran into criticism from veterans Wan Li, Bo Yibo, Yang Baibing, Wang Hanbing, Wang Enmao, and others.[20] They, with Qiao Shi, Wei Jianxing, and Li Ruihuan took umbrage at what they construed as Jiang's attempt to forge a cult of personality and to displace Deng's theories with his own. But at the summer Beidaihe retreat, Zhu Rongji for the first time endorsed Jiang's claim on both Party and CMC leadership positions.[21]

As late as the summer Beidaihe meetings preparatory to the 6th CC Plenum (September 2001), the presumption was still generational succession, as indicated by the preliminary slate approved there. The leaders publicly professed their support. Li Ruihuan, 67, proclaimed his intention to retire even though he had not yet reached the cutoff age, observing that in the Chang Jiang (Yangtze River), the waves behind drive on those ahead: "[W]e are old. We should let young people come forward. I believe that with the exception of Hu Jintao, all the standing committee members present at the meeting should step down. So should I." Zhu Rongj, attending the EU summit in Belgium in September 2001, said: "We should keep our promise to the whole Party. I am already old. I should completely step down.[22] Even Jiang, who had previously insisted (in a July 2000 conversation with visiting Japanese Prime Minister Keizo Obuchi) that the position of party secretary had no fixed tenure, declared during a September 4 visit to the Democratic People's Republic of Korea:

> The Party CC has a consensus, that is, that I and other members of the Politburo Standing Committee will quit completely. Some people within the Party have asked me to stay for one more term, there are also people asking the Premier to stay for one more term. We are all old. Of course we still have clear minds and still can work for 15–16 hours a day, but our retirement has been a foregone conclusion.[23]

While acknowledging the existence of a consensus, note that Jiang was still noncommittal about his own preference, observing that some wanted him to stay one more term, that although "we are old," he was still healthy and clear-minded and able to work prodigiously hard. Given numerous such opportunities, Jiang consistently refused to foreclose the possibility of an extension, usually evading the issue by replying that it will be settled according to CCP principles. He was also clearly interested in using proxies to ensure his access to the center.

Perhaps the best indication of Jiang's future ambitions at this time consisted of his growing interest in augmenting the CCP's doctrinal canon, thereby ranking along with Mao and Deng among China's great philosopher-kings. This began with the formulation of the "three emphases" (*san jiang*)—emphasize study, emphasize politics, and emphasize righteousness—introduced (with the assistance of Zeng Qinghong) in 1996 as a basis for the nationwide rectification of the Party, which lasted three years. The main focus of this campaign was on the second emphasis, "politics."[24] The three emphases should be distinguished from the more theoretically ambitious and politically consequential "Three Represents" (*sange daibia*), which state that the CCP represents society's most advanced productive forces, most advanced culture, and the interests of the broad masses—not just the classic Marxist proletariat, the workers and peasants. The political implications of the "Three Represents" were first spelled out in Jiang's speech commemorating the 80th anniversary of the Party's birth on July 1, 2001: Here Jiang proposed that the criteria for recruitment into the Party be broadened to include members of the middle, even the upper classes, conceivably including magnates like Henry Fok, the Macao

Casino tycoon.[25] Jiang expatiated on this formula in a series of talks, culminating in his remarks at the 6th Plenum of the 15th CC in September 2001: "The Communist Party should stick to Marxism-Leninism, Mao Zedong Thought and Deng Xiaoping Theory, and follow the Three Represents," the official Xinhua news agency admonished in its report.[26]

Such doctrinal innovations may have seemed jarring amid media reports that businesspeople had evaded more than 100 billion yuan of taxes in 2001, and in the context of the mounting industrial unemployment and rural discontent that would accompany China's preparations for entry into the World Trade Organization (WTO). And they raised a storm of controversy within the Party. This was mostly due to the ideological and sociological implications, but also because the adoption of the "Three Represents" would enhance Jiang's personal power base: If Jiang, like Mao, could define what is good and bad, right and wrong, he could also define *who* is right and wrong, good and bad. It became hard to tell to what extent the campaign represented an effort to broaden the class base of the Party and to what extent it was a litmus test for loyalty to Jiang, part of a new "personality cult." Indeed, media popularization of the "Three Represents" was typically accompanied by extravagant praise for their author.[27] By late 1999 the CC Secretariat had formed a committee to edit *The Selected Works of Jiang Zemin*, and by late 2001 compilation and editing had been completed, although publication was deferred pending convocation of the Party Congress. In Jiang's speech of May 31, 2002, at the Central Party School, he introduced a new formula for the new century, the "Three Stresses," that is, stress "on the overall situation, on unity and on stability." Although a full transcript of the speech has not been published, it reportedly contained criticism of unnamed "careerists and conspirators within the Party" who were failing to promote unity and national stability, while making nary a mention of "generational transition." The speech gave extra impetus to the nationwide campaign to promulgate Jiang's "Three Represents," which was duly enshrined in the Party statute at the 16th Congress—albeit without explicit reference to Jiang Zemin.[28] The words "revolutionary elements" were duly stricken, replacing them with "progressive elements from other social classes."

Meanwhile, in a series of meetings around the country starting in early January 2002, provincial Party leaders and leading military officials reportedly began calling on Jiang to stay on, for the sake of stability.[29] These calls were generally assumed to be orchestrated manifestations of loyalty by Jiang's protégés, whose careers might be jeopardized if Hu stepped in with his own claim on patronage spoils. The first step was for Jiang to stay on as CMC chairman by dint of the Deng Xiaoping precedent. But Jiang's military supporters contended that Jiang should retain Party leadership as well, lest the inexorable link between Party and gun be broken. Finally, according to a report in the Hong Kong media claiming to represent a leak from internal PRC documents, a new draft list of intended appointments was drawn up indicating that Jiang would not only be CMC chair, but also general secretary of the Party, thus remaining the "core" of the leadership and convener of the Politburo. Meanwhile, all mention of "generations" disappeared from the public media as of early 2002. This *bu tui* option would eliminate the hypocrisy and doctrinal incongruence involved in ruling the Party from the PLA, at the price of violating the age limit adopted to eliminate Qiao Shi in 1997.

The next thrust in this seesaw succession struggle would be delivered by the Party veterans, at the closed high-level meetings held at the Beidaihe resort in July–August 2002. Having ultimately agreed to step down, the old guard (including Bo Yibo) could see no reason for Jiang Zemin to stay on, and wrote a letter to the Politburo Standing Committee in ardent support of Deng Xiaoping's goal of eliminating lifetime tenure. The leadership agreed, noting that Jiang's promise would not be too meaningful if he did not completely retire, and that if special provision were made for him to continue in office this would logically have to be extended to Li Peng, Zhu Rongji, and perhaps others as well. Jiang voiced no objection at the time, winning support for his slate for the next Politburo. Then, at a Politburo meeting convened October 16, just before Jiang's trip to Crawford, he unleashed an assault on his old rival Li Ruihuan, otherwise slated to move into the number-two ranking and chair the NPC. Noting that Li had over the past several months repeatedly offered to retire early, Jiang observed that this would be good for the Party's rejuvenation. Zeng had helpfully collected "evidence" of Li's "lifestyle" problems, including an older brother who was accused of "corruption" for using his *guanxi* (connection) in pursuit of good property development deals, and an alleged liaison with a movie star. Having secured agreement for Li's dismissal, Jiang proposed that Li be replaced by Jia Qinglin and that the new age of retirement for Politburo members be set at 68; both suggestions were quickly adopted.

Then, at the first plenum of a freshly elected twenty-four–member Politburo cleared of all those who had previously embarrassed Jiang on this issue, several members reportedly pointed out that despite the need for rejuvenation, the PLA needed an experienced leader at its helm in view of the complicated situation across the Taiwan Strait, as well unstable Sino-American relations. In the official information given to the delegates to the 16th Party Congress, Hu Jintao had been the only candidate for the post of CMC chair, as all other members of the previous Standing Committee (including Jiang) had retired from the CC. But the Politburo quickly ratified the proposal that Jiang retain chairmanship of the CMC by simple voice vote, Hu Jintao having raised no objections. Jiang also delivered the report to the congress, and was most prominently featured in the media and even listed first in the protocol ranking (with Hu as number two); this will reportedly remain true until Jiang steps down from the presidency in March 2003, at which point he will drop to second place. As CMC chairman he will, however, continue to be privy to the paper flow for all Politburo Standing Committee proceedings, and Hu has promised in (leaked) internal Party meetings that Jiang will continue to be consulted on major decisions prior to Politburo sessions. The rest of the retiring Standing Committee members will also continue to be copied on Standing Committee communications until March, at which point they will be cut out of the paper flow, leaving only Jiang.[30] It had been speculated that Jiang would retain CMC chairmanship only until March, retiring from both state and party CMC chairmanships (whose memberships are identical) at the same time that he relinquishes his term-limited position as state president.[31] But Jiang has subsequently made clear in conversations with foreign visitors that he means to stay on for at least two or three years, possibly five.[32]

Implications for Post-Jiang Politics

What difference does this ambiguous, quasi succession make politically? Very little, with regard to policy—Hu Jintao has been at pains to manifest his agreement with Jiang's policy positions. Procedurally the situation is more complicated. The fact that it does not represent as much progress as the advocates of "generational succession" had hoped for should not obscure the fact that it does represent more limited progress in the same general direction. While Jiang has used Deng's precedent as a pretext to resist further movement, if he does in fact remain the sole exception to retirement based on age limits, this does represent institutional progress from the 14th and 15th Congresses, which allowed an entire cohort of senior leaders (the so-called "sitting committee") to remain politically influential. Moreover, this is the first time that the Party Congress will have elected a new Party secretary general since the 6th Party Congress in 1928, which decided (with the help of the Comintern) on a young peasant named Xiang Zhongfa, who was then promptly eclipsed by the fiery labor organizer Li Lisan. An informal "regency" has been institutionalized, and the rules governing the heir apparent (get the regent's approval for all decisions) have been made more explicit (Zhao leaked this rule only when facing a critical decision in May 1989, fatally embarrassing his patron).

Jiang's sham retirement paradoxically marks his political zenith, in terms of political horse-trading and informal personal power. After years of being thwarted in pushing his appointments through, Zeng is promoted to the Politburo Standing Committee and Li Ruihuan is purged, and the new lineup is more lopsidedly composed of Jiang's protégés than its predecessor. In addition, the "Three Represents" becomes Party doctrine and Jiang's selected works (*Jiang Zemin Talks Socialism with Chinese Characteristics*) are published, elevating Jiang to the same empyrean status as Deng or Mao. And, as a political manipulator, he may in fact be their equal. Jiang is after all no charismatic leader—any proclivity for transformational leadership would have disqualified him in the era of institutionalizing reform. In the vein of Deng's "black cat, white cat," Jiang has become identified with the mantra, "stability takes priority over everything." In view of the fact that his successor has been at great pains to demonstrate complete accord with established policy preferences, it becomes harder to justify a procedural exception than might have been in the case of a transformational leader leading permanent revolution. Jiang's only argument in support of his exemption was that the international environment was vaguely threatening, which posed a challenge that transactional leadership and institutionalized rule might not be able to meet. Unlike the revolutionary era, there seems to be no suitably meretricious task whereby a succeeding technocratic leader can appropriately acquit himself. That Jiang's paradoxical or even contradictory argument proved persuasive is perhaps attributable to extralogical factors. Like his predecessors, Jiang shrewdly realized that his own retirement was his biggest bargaining chip in gaining his colleagues' consent; thus, Jiang exchanged his prospective retirement for concessions on appointments of his proxies to various strategic positions to safeguard his legacy—and then at the last moment rescinded his pledge to retire.

Despite the enshrinement of the "Three Represents," Jiang's exceptionalism represents perhaps a re-personalization of power rather than a return to the ideological politics of the Maoist era. The difference between winners and losers at the 16th Congress was not based on ideological or policy cleavages (of which there is no evidence), but on their ties to a powerful patron. We seem to have personalism at the top, and technocracy everywhere else. Although policy change has been minimized, there are two conceivable policy impacts. The factional impact at the top conforms to Tang Tsou's model of "a game to win all or to lose all," that is, Jiang's faction emerges supreme, more than ever the "mainstream" faction. Having thus consolidated his power, Jiang now retires (only) in favor of those he wants. Consequently, Hu Jintao's heir apparency is not only postponed, but becomes more ambiguous, in the light of the simultaneous rise of Zeng Qinghong, and possibly others. Although the reported *quid pro quo* Hu demanded for his concurrence with Jiang's last-minute comeback was Jiang's support for his deferred succession, he may well wonder: Will Jiang change his mind about stepping down in 2007 as he changed his mind in 2002? Instead of helping Hu consolidate his heir apparency as Deng had for Jiang in 1989–1994, will Jiang play Mao's old game and balance Hu against Zeng, Wu, or Huang?

Will reform survive the departure of Zhu Rongji? For the past several years, Jiang Zemin has worked in tandem with Zhu in pressing for China's admission to the WTO and in the implementation of economic reform, swinging from Zhu back to Li Peng to crush Falun Gong, or when Zhu advocated political or media reforms. Zhu was brilliant, principled, and energetic, but never suffered fools gladly, and aroused resentment from those whose interests were damaged by the reforms (including unemployed workers and peasants). And Zhu was willing to take the heat for economic reform's collateral damage. Wen Jiabao, his chosen heir, has a reputation as a much "rounder" operator, a second Zhou Enlai, who does not provoke such intense ambivalence—but Wen may not push reform as energetically as Zhu in the face of bureaucratic vested interests, particularly given Jiang's propensity to retreat in the face of perceived risks. But if we assume Wen will be an equally effective advocate of Zhu's portfolio, the prognosis is an extension of the post-Tiananmen consensus; that is, economic but not political reform, with greater impact on personnel balance than on the policy mix.

The foreign policy impact of the adjusted scenario may be salubrious, permitting a battle-tested and still-vigorous foreign policy leadership to continue in a mentoring role, while permitting the fourth-generation leadership, hitherto lacking much exposure to the world stage, to acquire the necessary poise to take the helm. Hu Jintao spent most of his career as a Party functionary; except for a brief trip to Japan in early 1998 he had not been outside the country until 2001, when he undertook a tour of five European nations, followed by a visit to the United States in spring 2002. Nor has Wen Jiabao held a diplomatic or national security portfolio throughout his career. Most of Hu's young protégés in the CYL faction are also Party functionaries with exclusively domestic experience. As Jiang has agreed to retire from formal membership in the Politburo (indeed, the CC itself), he will also retire from the CC's "small groups," such as the Foreign Affairs Leadership Small Group or the Taiwan Affairs Small Group (both of which he formerly chaired), leaving much of the foreign policy leadership in transition. Qian Qichen, the so-called godfather of modern Chinese diplomacy, has also retired due to age limits. Foreign Minister Tang Jiaxhuan also retired when a new State Council cabinet was formed in March 2003. Tang committed a diplomatic gaffe when he claimed in public in 2001 that managing the political repercussions of Taiwan's 2000 election was a primary achievement of the foreign ministry. (Watching the news conference, Qian reportedly shook his head and said, "This is going to be a problem.") Prime candidates to succeed Tang included Vice Foreign Minister (and former ambassador to the United States) Li Zhaoxing as well as Liu Huaqiu and Dai Bingguo, and Li finally became the minister. Since late 2000 there has been talk in Beijing that Jiang wanted to set up a National Security Council of China (NSCC), more powerful than its U.S. counterpart, centralizing control over public and state security agencies and armed police, the chairmanship of which might have formalized Jiang's continuing influence in foreign affairs. But when after a series of discussions it was decided that membership would be reserved to acting Politburo members, Jiang lost interest in the scheme and it has gone nowhere. If it is revived under different ground rules, it may be a route for Jiang and the "elders" to reassert authority over security and foreign affairs.

Conclusion

Although it would certainly be premature to draw firm conclusions from an analysis of a process so recently concluded, this may be a good scholarly opportunity to reconsider some old problems in Chinese politics in the light of new but still tentative empirical findings. Two problem areas seem particularly relevant: first, the problem of informal politics and its relationship to formal structure. Second, the problem in a dictatorship (of the people!) is how to transfer power from one all-powerful leader to another in a context of political institutionalization without some erosion of aggregate power.

The Jiang regime represents deepening economic reform, deferred political reform, and continuation of the long march toward formal institutionalization: Whereas Deng retired formally in 1987, then again (more thoroughly) in 1989, he did not cede his informal influence until physically incapacitated in late 1994. His long, ambivalent effort to step down while remaining at the power center resulted in a yawning gulf between formal and informal power, as formal leaders became marionettes of their senior patrons. This was nowhere more manifest than in the Tiananmen decision, of which we now have a good record, when Deng and his fellow veterans completely overrode the Politburo Standing Committee.[33] Jiang Zemin has been able to bring formal and informal power back into much closer alignment, in part by dint of his skillful ingratiation of the surviving seniors (most of whom eventually died off), and in part by concentrating formal and informal power in his own hands.

It would be tempting to infer from the successful realignment of formal and informal politics that factionalism has been eliminated, and it does seem to be true that at least at the top level, factionalism has lost much of its erstwhile intensity. Factional coalitions tend to be shallower and more fluid; thus Jiang Zemin in the early 1990s was close to Li Peng, while since the 15th Congress he has worked more closely with Zhu Rongji to prepare China for entry into the WTO (which Li opposed), although he abandoned Zhu to join Li in the crackdown on the Falun Gong. Whereas it is clear from the recent maneuvers over succession that factionalism has not disappeared, it has changed its form. Factions no longer seem to be organized around ideological "lines," as during the late Maoist period, nor around policy platforms, as they were during the Deng Xiaoping era (e.g., the "whateverists" vs. "pragmatists," then the radical reformers vs. the moderate reformers). Thus, it is rather striking in the succession maneuvers how little these have involved the articulation of policy issues. To be sure, there are still some ardent leftists, notably Deng Liqun and his coterie, and some dedicated liberals, especially among intellectuals, but for the most part these voices have been marginalized. Jiang's achievement has been to create at the center a reformist middle-of-the road consensus, about which no debate is conceivable. Instead, factional groupings tend to revolve around a vague mixture of common geographic origin and personal ties. They appear to play little role in the policymaking process, while remaining significant in personnel policy.

The run-up to the 16th Congress succession conformed to the old "succession crisis" syndrome in the sense that there was pervasive uncertainty, an increase in factional maneuvers, and a postponement of strategic decisions (such decisions presuppose an answer to the question of who makes them). In this sense, many of the apparent gains of institutionalization have already been undone by the controversy. Yet there have been significant differences from the PRC's previous successions. Jiang Zemin emerged as a stronger and more durable successor than Hua Guofeng, to whom he is sometimes compared, for several reasons. Hua had important constraints on his power: His endorsement by Mao Zedong imposed constraints on his policy entrepreneurship, and he was boxed in by threats from both left (the Gang of Four) and right (Deng Xiaoping, Chen Yun). In comparison, Jiang also inherited the liability of Tiananmen from his predecessor, forcing him to defend an unpopular decision (June 4, vs. April 5 for Hua) and to continue to criticize a popular deposed politician (Zhao Ziyang for Jiang, vs. Deng Xiaoping for Hua). However, Deng's pragmatism allowed ample latitude for innovative interpretation, of which Jiang and Zhu took full advantage to deepen marketization, even though Qiao Shi and other critics also exploited this latitude to offer competing interpretations. Jiang dealt with the Tiananmen legacy essentially by putting it on the back burner. His criticisms of Zhao were relatively mild and restrained, in contrast to Hua's unforgiving campaign against Deng. It remains to be seen whether Jiang will help Hu to come into his own or block him as a threat to his own continued political ambitions, but the initial outlook is not in my judgment very encouraging.

In his campaign to escape the leadership's institutionalized succession scenario, Jiang found himself hoist by his own petard. Having brought formal and informal politics back into alignment, he was reluctant to disassemble them. Thus, complete retirement, Deng Xiaoping's role after 1989, was not an attractive option for Jiang. It was incompatible with the combination of the unprecedented power he was able to accrue as a price for stepping down and his own irrepressible love for political eminence. The notion of Jiang as China's George Washington, who self-effacingly retires to set a precedent for posterity, is probably beyond Jiang's conceptual vocabulary—this is after all a transactional leader par excellence, not a charismatic visionary. Jiang's choice suggests that the realm of informal politics in China has been shrinking. If we survey the landscape for retired but still politically active veterans, we find that oldsters like Deng Liqun and Qiao Shi have continued to wield a certain informal power without portfolio, but then they never had the power of a paramount leader and could not function as kingmakers (or king breakers). Thus, the sharp disjunction between formal and informal power that has long marked CCP politics, allowing informal elites to intervene at will and upstage formal authorities (as they did at Tiananmen), may be in remission. Of course, this only applies to the relationship between role and authority; the rules themselves (including role expectations) appear to remain relatively informal— meaning *personal*, depending on who makes them, under what political circumstances, and for whom. Again, this is only at the very top; elsewhere, institutionalization is increasingly taking effect.

Notes

I am grateful to Kun-Chin Lin for his invaluable research assistance and to the Center for Chinese Studies of the University of California at Berkeley for financial support. For their helpful comments on an earlier draft of this article, I am particularly indebted to Kun-Chin Lin, Gang Lin, Xuezhi Guo, and Xiaobo Hu.

1. A good synopsis of Deng's reforms of the succession process may be found in Peter N.S. Lee, "The Informal Politics of Leadership Succession in Post-Mao China," in *Informal Politics in East Asia*, ed. Lowell Dittmer, Haruhiro Fukui, and Peter N.S. Lee (N.Y.: Cambridge University Press, 2000), 165–183.

2. See Melanie Manion, *Retirement of Revolutionaries in China: Public Policies, Social Norms, Private Interests* (Princeton, N.J.: Princeton University Press, 1993).

3. For example, in early 1997, NPC representatives registered high levels of dissatisfaction with the annual work reports delivered by the Supreme People's Procurator and the Supreme People's Court, with a record number of abstentions and negative votes. The NPC thrice rejected the State Council's fuel tax, and has spearheaded efforts to centralize and introduce greater transparency to bureaucratic accounting, budgetary, and information-gathering procedures; see *Cheng Ming* (Hong Kong), April 1997, p. 56. On the fuel tax, see Kun-Chin Lin, "Markets and Hierarchies in Post-Socialism: Theory and Evidence from the Chinese Oil Industry" (paper presented at Annual Meeting of the American Political Science Association, San Francisco, Calif., September 1, 2001). The CPPCC has also demonstrated greater activism since the 15th Congress, in particular since 2001, when it has become a center of criticism of Jiang's ideological innovations.

4. For instance, Liaoning Governor Bo Xilai (son of Bo Yibo) and Henan Governor Li Keqiang are both Peking University alumni. Shanxi Party Secretary Tian Chengping, Shandong Party Secretary Wu Guanzheng, Fujian Governor Xi Jinping, and Yunnan Governor Xu Rongkai are Tsinghua University graduates.

5. *Wen Wei Po* (Hong Kong), December 31, 2001, p. A3; *Ming Pao* (Hong Kong), January 17, 2002, p. B14; Si Liang, "China Makes Earnest Preparations for 16th Party Congress to Be Held in Second Half of This Year," *Zhongguo Tongxun She* (Hong Kong), January 7, 2002.

6. Peng Kailei and Ma Haiyan, "Turnover of Top Provincial and Municipal Officials to Greet 16th CPC Congress," *Wen Wei Po* (Hong Kong), March 2, 2002, p. A5.

7. The alternate is Zhang Ruimin, chief executive officer of Haier Corporation, Shandong Province.

8. *Ming Pao*, October 6, 2001, p. B13.

9. Oliver Chou, "Rising Up the PLA Ranks," *South China Morning Post*, April 25,

2002; Xia Wensi, "Jiang Zemin Intends to Let Zeng Qinghong Assume Military Power," *Kai Fang* (Hong Kong), January 1, 2002, pp. 11–13.

10. Willy Wo-Lap Lam, CNN, November 22, 2002, available at www.cnn.com, accessed on November 22, 2002.

11. "Special Dispatch: Young Cadres Will Be Selected to Head Provinces and Ministries," *Ming Pao*, November 4, 2000; *Sing Tao Jih Pao* (Hong Kong), April 9, 2001.

12. "Beijing Grapevine Full of Rumors about Jiang and Li's Future," *Sing Tao Jih Pao*, January 10, 2001, p. A14; *Kai Fang*, November 2000, p. 13. *Cheng Ming* editors concluded, however, that Zeng's factional constituency was stronger than Hu's; see *Cheng Ming*, July 2002, pp. 38–40.

13. See Cheng Li, *China's Leaders: The New Generation* (Lanham, Md.: Rowman and Littlefield, 2001), chapter 4.

14. The four provincial party secretaries promoted to the Politburo Standing Committee were Wu Guanzheng, Shandong; Huang Ju, Shanghai; Li Changchun, Guangdong; and Jia Qinglin, Beijing. Eight other provincial Party secretaries were appointed to the Politburo, including Wang Lequan (Xinjiang), Hui Liangyu (Jiangsu), Liu Qi (Beijing), Zhang Lichang (Tianjin), Zhang Dejiang (Zhejiang), Chen Liangyu (Shanghai), Zhou Yongkang (Sichuan), and Yu Zhengsheng (Hubei).

15. On transformational and transactional leadership, see James MacGregor Burns, *Leadership* (N. Y.: Harper & Row, 1978). Burns's assessment of transformational leadership is far more sanguine than that of most Chinese who experienced the Cultural Revolution.

16. Touring the country in 1999, Qiao Shi cited Deng's call (in a talk in Guangdong) for elderly cadres to retire after two terms, and disclosed the details of his own retirement in 1997 as part of an "arrangement" whereby all senior cadres would step down when their time came.

17. *Cheng Ming*, August 1999, pp. 16–17.

18. Ibid., pp. 18–19. Deng Liqun actually found seven sins in Deng Xiaoping's theories: (1) betraying Marxism; (2) bringing internal decay to the Party; (3) destroying the faith and belief in the Party; (4) dissipating the Party's ability to mobilize the masses; (5) generating tension and hostility between the Party, the state, and the masses; (6) polarizing income distribution, and thus intensifying social contradictions; and (7) completely undermining the advantages of socialism.

19. *Cheng Ming*, December 1999, pp. 12–13.

20. *Cheng Ming*, July 2000, pp. 14–16.

21. *Cheng Ming*, September 2000, p. 10.

22. Xia, "Jiang Zemin."

23. Lo Ping, "Jiang Zemin Verbally Confers Title of 'Principal Core' [zhuti hexin] on Hu, Zeng," *Cheng Ming*, October 1, 2001, pp. 12–13.

24. "Emphasizing politics" turned out to involve outside work teams encouraging grassroots workers and peasants to openly criticize their local leaders. When the campaign was taken to China's less prosperous regions, particularly in the countryside, the resulting upsurge of criticism turned out to be quite explosive. Accompanying a work team on a February 25, 2000, visit to the backwater Gaozhou region of Guangdong Province, Jiang, when confronted by such negative feedback, improvised the "Three Represents" formula: "Summarizing the more than 70-year history of our Party, an important conclusion can be reached, that is, our Party won the support of the people because throughout the historical stages of revolution, construction and reform, our Party

has always represented (1) the developmental demands of China's advanced productivity, (2) the forward direction of China's advanced culture and (3) the fundamental interests of China's broad masses." Su Shaozhi, "Critiquing the 'Three Represents' Theory," *Cheng Ming*, July 2000, pp. 45–53.

25. For a close textual analysis of the July 1 talk, see *Chung Kung Yen Chiu* (Taipei), September 2001, pp. 1–9.

26. Peter Harmsen, Agence France Presse, September 27, 2001.

27. See *Chung Kung Yen Chiu*, September 2001, pp. 1–9.

28. John Pomfret, "Chinese Leader Throws a Curve: Jiang's Reluctance to Retire Could Spark Power Struggle," *Washington Post*, July 21, 2002, p. A01; Willy Wo-Lap Lam, CNN, July 28, 2002, available at www.cnn.com, accessed on July 28, 2002.

29. See Pomfret, "Chinese Leader Throws a Curve." See also Hiroyuki Sugiyama, in *Yomiuri Shimbun* (Tokyo), June 21, 2002. Although these reports cannot be independently confirmed, it seems plausible that faced with widespread expectations that he should retire, Jiang would prefer to orchestrate grassroots demands rather than simply announce his intention not to do so.

30. Susan Lawrence, "One Leader Too Many," *Far Eastern Economic Review*, November 28, 2002, pp. 28–32.

31. See Andrew Nathan and Bruce Gilley, "China's New Rulers: 1. The Path to Power," *New York Review of Books*, September 26, 2002; and Nathan and Gilley, "China's New Rulers: What They Want," *New York Review of Books*, October 10, 2002.

32. Lawrence, "One Leader Too Many."

33. See Zhang Liang, *The Tiananmen Papers*. ed. Andrew J. Nathan and Perry Link, with an afterword by Orville Schell (N.Y.: Public Affairs, 2001). For my review, see *China Quarterly*, no. 166 (2001): 476–484.

Chapter 2

Ideology and Political Institutions for a New Era

Gang Lin

Despite Beijing's de-emphasis on communist doctrine and its concentration on economic development from two decades ago, ideology still plays an indispensable role in Chinese society in general and political institutions in particular. Since spring 2000, the Chinese Communist Party (CCP) has been engaged in an ideological campaign advancing a new theoretical motif of "Three Represents," a significant move heralding China's transition toward the post-Jiang era.[1] Literally, the "Three Represents" formula means that the CCP should "always represent the developmental requirement of China's advanced productive forces, represent the developing orientation of China's advanced culture, and represent the fundamental interests of the overwhelming majority of the Chinese people." Ideologically, the essence of this new concept is to redefine the Party as an ever-innovating organization corresponding to China's ongoing socioeconomic and cultural changes, with its ruling constituency (*zhizheng jichu*) being expanded from the working class to the general public.

It is difficult to overstate the tremendous influence of such a new ideological framework on Chinese politics, given the half-totalitarian and half-authoritarian characteristics of the current regime.[2] The implications of "Three Represents" for leadership succession that perpetuate Jiang's political influence in the post-Jiang China were mentioned in Chapter 1. The following two chapters touch on the political impact of such an idea on China's new property rights system and changing state–society relations. This chapter explores the linkage between this theoretical innovation (*lilun chuangxin*) and institutional innovation (*zhidu chuangxin*) in the post-Jiang era, focusing on China's political reform. Questions to be examined here include: How likely and to what extent will the Party redefine itself from the vanguard of the working class to a new organization representing the general public? If so, what would be the political implications of such an ideological change for the Party's internal structure and its ruling style? In what ways will the Party resolve the tension between the principle of majority rule and that of democratic centralism? To what degree will the fourth generation of leaders expand the "intra-party democracy" (*dangnei minzhu*) to the whole society through "institutionalization, standardization and procedural formalization (*zhiduhua, guifanhua, chengxuhua*) of socialist democracy?"[3] What are the constraints of the old system on China's political reform?

Just like leadership transition during which the formal process is overshadowed by informal politics, political institutions in China are far from formalization. In the absence of free and competitive elections for government officials, institutional innovation by the Party elite is inevitably constrained by the dominant system of socialism and one-Party rule. By analyzing the political elite's diversified and changeable interests and their ability to renovate the old ideology and institutions without overhauling the whole system, this chapter attempts to shed light on the prospect of political reform in post-Jiang China.

Searching for New Legitimacy

Amid an increasingly market-oriented pluralistic society and a mounting identity crisis, the CCP has started "searching aggressively for a new set of principles and policies" to ensure its survival since the dawn of this century.[4] In a similar way of reinterpreting Chinese socialism pragmatically to accommodate the reality of a market economy (as Deng Xiaoping did a decade earlier), the Party now attempts to redefine its legitimacy and modernize itself in a more diversified society. The advancement of the "Three

Represents" idea therefore reflects the Party's new effort to reconcile its traditional doctrine with changing society in the wake of China's two decades of reform and openness. As one article published in the Shanghai-based *Jiefang Ribao* (Liberation Daily) claims, the "Three Represents" idea closely keeps pace with the times and constitutes an ideological system for handling the most acute, sensitive, realistic, and conspicuous issues within the Party. Theoretically, the article goes on to say, to represent the advanced productive forces ensures the Party's ruling credentials, to represent advanced culture enhances the Party's ruling capability, and to represent the fundamental interests of the overwhelming majority of the Chinese people provides a solid ruling constituency for the Party.[5] In the words of Jiang Zemin, "Persistent implementation of the 'Three Represents' is the foundation for building our Party (*lidang zhiben*), the cornerstone for its governance (*zhizheng zhiji*), and the source of its strength (*liliang zhiyuan*)."[6]

Party Legitimacy Redefined

Over the past half-century, the CCP's ruling legitimacy has been frequently challenged by Chinese society, as highlighted by the out-of-control "Hundred Flowers" campaign in the 1950s, the chaotic Cultural Revolution between the 1960s and 1970s, pro-democracy student movements in the 1980s, and radical nationalism since the 1990s. Meanwhile, the Party's identity has also experienced subtle changes. During the Mao era, the CCP was defined as the vanguard of the proletariat, representing the advanced forces and relations of production (*shengchanli he shengchan guangxi*).[7] The Party claimed its ruling legitimacy that was supported by a remote communist goal, past revolutionary experiences, continued political campaigns and "thought reeducation," and a centrally commanded socialist economy dominated by state-run enterprises. In the post-Mao era, the Chinese government began "to shift the base of Party legitimacy from virtue to competence."[8] The Party rebuilt its legitimacy based on the so-called one center (giving top priority to economic development) and "two basic points" (adhere to reform and openness, and adhere to the "four cardinal principles"—Party leadership, socialist road, proletarian dictatorship, and Marxism, Leninism, and Mao Zedong thought).

To defend and reinterpret socialism in the reform era amid the wave of global democratization, the reform elite led by Deng fought against both the "rightist" and "leftist" tendencies within and outside the Party. On the one hand, the Party advanced a series of campaigns to defend socialism and attack the "rightist" liberals, such as "antibourgeois liberalization" in 1981 and 1986–1987, "antispiritual pollution" in 1983–1984, and "anti-imperialist peaceful evolution" and post-Tiananmen re-education in 1989–1991. On the other hand, the Party promoted several thought emancipation (*sixiang jiefang*) movements to reform the socialist system. Following the creative theoretical discourse on the "primary stage" of Chinese socialism at the 13th Party Congress in 1987, a well-known ideological debate on the basic functions and identity (*xingzhi*) of the market economy took place in 1992, when leftist ideologues wanted to preserve a pure "socialist planned economy," and pragmatic reformers sought to develop an ideology-free market economy. Another debate around property rights reform in 1997 involved leftists who gave priority to preserving state ownership and reformers who preferred efficiency to the form of ownership.[9]

A significant trend going through these theoretical debates since the post-Mao era is that leftists have dramatically lost their offensive momentum and became a small group of hapless defenders of the dogmatic socialism. While leftists in the Mao era were conceptually associated with radicals who dreamed of dragging China into a communist society overnight, they are perceived as conservative ideologues in the post-Mao era. Such a perceptual change displays a vivid picture that communism in China today is at low ebb. Contrary to its heyday during the Great Leap Forward under Mao, the communist blueprint has been relegated to a remote future hundreds or even thousands years away from now.[10] Such a theoretical shift demonstrates the changing interest of the Party elite and its ability to adapt to the new environment by reinterpreting socialism within the existing ideological framework.

By reinterpreting Chinese socialism to accommodate an emergent market economy that incorporates both the state and the non-state sectors, the Party has promised to deliver prosperity and wealth to all people while allowing for a certain degree of distributive inequality among them. The advancement of the "Three Represents" suggests that the Party is abandoning its ideological preference for state enterprises, whose problems with inefficiency and bankruptcy can no longer justify state ownership as necessarily the most advanced system. This does not mean, however, that the Party has acknowledged the non-state sectors as more efficient than the state sector. Rather, by referring to the "developmental requirement of China's advanced productive forces" without mentioning the "productive relationship," the Party elite encourages the coexistence of different sectors as long as they can promote the development of the advanced productive forces (gauged by the level of scientific technology). As Jiang Zemin announced in his report to the 16th National Party Congress, "All work that contributes to the socialist modernization drive in China, physical or mental, and simple or complicated, is glorious and should be acknowledged and respected . . . All legitimate income, from labor or not, should be protected."[11] Such a theoretical innovation demonstrates that the legal income from capital is no longer ideologically discriminated against by the Party. In the mind-set of Party leaders, economic prosperity will not only win credit for the ruling Party, but will also neutralize income gaps between rich and poor and thwart social protests. In other words, continued economic growth is one of the principal sources of the regime's legitimacy, a lesson the Party elite learned from the chaotic Cultural Revolution.

Shifts of Ruling Constituencies

As mentioned earlier, the CCP used to define itself as the vanguard of the proletariat, with the majority of its members being workers and peasants, led by the revolutionary elite. Since the beginning of economic reform and openness, the Party has gradually transformed itself from a revolutionary party into a ruling party, redefining itself as the vanguard of the working class. The working class, according to Beijing's new definition, includes industrial workers, intellectuals, managers for state-owned enterprises, and officials/staff in the Party and the government.[12] This term is more inclusive than the Marxist definition of the proletariat. By claiming intellectuals as part of the working class, the Chinese political elite expanded its constituencies by recruiting the intellectual elite into the Party.

The advancement of the "Three Represents" is another strategic move by the Party to recruit the economic elite, particularly those private entrepreneurs who are not included in the category of the working class. This theoretical innovation, aimed at redefining Party identity, was inspired by the fact that many private entrepreneurs had already joined the Party at the local level before Jiang initiated the "Three Represents" idea in spring 2000.[13] Even so, the idea of allowing private entrepreneurs to join the Party fomented a new ideological debate within the Party. While the reform elite wanted to breathe new life into some of the Party's stale Marxist dogmas, the leftists attacked Jiang's "Three Represents" for changing the identity of the Party. To reduce the shock, Jiang took an ambiguous strategy, and made a theoretical distinction between the identity of the Party and its mass base (*qunzhong jichu*). According to his argument, the Party was still the vanguard of the working class, and the recruitment of private entrepreneurs into the Party was aimed at expanding the Party's mass base.[14] At the same time, Jiang made it clear that the Party was the vanguard not only for the working class, but also for all the Chinese people and the Chinese nation. Such strategic ambiguity in redefining the Party was the result of political compromise between traditional ideologues and the reform elite.

As expected, the 16th National Congress of the CCP enshrined the "Three Represents" formula in the Party constitution. For the first time, private entrepreneurs were selected to participate in the congress.[15] While repeating that the Party is always the vanguard of the working class, the Party now actually highlights itself as the vanguard for the Chinese people—including the working class, the peasantry, individual businesspeople, private entrepreneurs, and other social strata. However, given social polarization in today's China, the political implication of such a theoretical innovation is that the Party will become a more elitist-oriented organization, with a new trinity of political (officials), economic (entrepreneurs and managers), and intellectual elites at its top level.

Political Culture Rejuvenated

Chinese reformers realize that as the CCP has been transformed from a revolutionary party into a ruling party, its ruling platform and style must be reformed to adapt to the market and economic globalization. In a related fashion, Chinese political culture must also be rejuvenated (*zhengzhi wenhua gengxin*) to adapt to a new international order supported by political mutual trust, economic cooperation, and cultural exchange.[16] Reformers believe that China's entry into the World Trade Organization (WTO) requires that the country play by the international rules of the game (*yu guoji jiegui*), transform traditional government functions, and speed up the process of establishing a socialist legal state combining the rule of law (*yifa zhiguo*, which literally means ruling according to the law) and the rule by virtue (*yide zhiguo*). One Chinese scholar even argues that the CCP can adopt certain useful mechanisms practiced in Western political parties and parliaments, without simply copying any country's political system.[17]

This theoretical discourse displays a significant departure from traditional Marxist doctrine. In the past, the CCP always denounced liberal democracy as either a hypocritical showcase of the bourgeoisie or irrelevant to China's unique national circumstances. In the name of proletarian democracy, the Party claimed that the socialist political system in China was superior to Western democracies. Since the beginning of the reform era, the CCP has often emphasized "China's unique national circumstances" as a legitimate reason for rejecting liberal democracy. As the theory of proletarian democracy lost its appeal to the ordinary Chinese people, proponents of neo-authoritarianism emerged—in nonofficial discourse—to fill in the ideological vacuum in the late 1980s, arguing that China needs a strong government to promote market reform first and then reach the goal of liberal democracy. In the wake of the 1989 Tiananmen incident, neo-authoritarianism was replaced by neo-conservatism supported by the stability-above-all mentality. Both neo-conservatism and the official ideology disregarded Western democratic experience as applicable to China.

In contrast, liberalism has gradually resurrected since the mid-1990s, when political scientists began to advocate the idea of limited governance related to a market economy. In a book published by the Central Party School Press, Wang Jingsong argued a limited government could successfully reach its goals, and institutional checks and balances should be established within the government.[18] In a similar vein, other scholars argued that "democratic and legal construction" required limitations on the powers of government and political leaders.[19] Toward the end of the 1990s, a number of intellectuals had put forward a series of democratic ideas in public discourse ranging from protection of private property rights, limited government, rule of law, political accountability, to direct elections of state leadership.[20] Probably inspired by this discourse, one liberal scholar acclaimed "a quiet comeback of liberalism" to China.[21]

However, the development of liberalism in China is still constrained by official ideology, which Chinese intellectuals cannot openly challenge. For example, the idea of multiparty electoral competition for political leadership is still inhibited in academic discussion. While liberalism is unlikely to become China's ideological mainstream in the short run, its growing appeal to Chinese intellectuals has raised a new issue for the ruling Party as to how to define the "orientation of China's advanced culture." Jiang Zemin tried to answer this question in his speech during ceremonies of the 80th anniversary of the CCP on July 1, 2001. On the one hand, he argued that diverse civilizations and social systems in the world should coexist, and that peoples under different social systems could learn from each other. On the other hand, he insisted on the principle of democratic centralism, calling on the Party to firmly resist the influence of Western political models on China, such as the multiparty system (*duodangzhi*) and the division of powers among executive, legislative, and judicial branches (*sanquan dingli*).

Interestingly, in his May 31, 2002, speech at the Central Party School, Jiang changed his tone by saying that China should develop its own unique socialist democracy, and "never copy any models of the political system of the West." One can find some nuances between Jiang's two speeches. The replacement of "firmly resist" (*jianjue dizhi*) with "never copy" (*juebu zhaobang*) suggests the Party's softening hostility toward the Western political system. Also, in his May 31 speech, Jiang called on the Party to develop socialist political civilization (*zhengzhi wenming*) in China. According to Chinese scholars' interpretation, the new concept of "socialist political civilization" contains several points. First, political civilization is part of the civilization of humankind; and advanced political civilization includes progressive political ideas, such as democracy, liberty, equality, fairness, justice, political transparency, and human rights, which are shared by all human beings. Second, the development of socialist democracy in China should correspond to the country's economic and social development as well as its political tradition, and China should never copy any Western political models. Third, in promoting political development, China can learn from the achievements of political civilization of other peoples, including *some elements* (emphasis added by author) of Western democracy in terms of theoretical principles, instiutional design, and political process. Fourth, the priority in developing political civilization is to ensure that China's socialist democracy is institutionalized and standardized, with corresponding procedures.[22] Such a theoretical innovation suggests Beijing's flexibility and bottom line in search for the socialist democracy in general and intra-party democracy in particular.

Developing Intra-Party Democracy

The changing identity of the Party as well as the Chinese society has presented a new challenge to the CCP in terms of its old ruling style guided by Leninist democratic centralism. During the Mao era, the CCP ruled China through economic monopoly, ideological mobilization, class struggle, and proletarian dictatorship. Correspondingly, Mao served as a patriarchal leader within the Party, free of institutional and disciplinary constraints. After Mao, Deng attempted to develop socialist democracy and the legal system through power decentralization (*fenquan*), administrative reform, village autonomy, and building the legal system, while maintaining the Party's leadership. Deng also sought to establish intra-party democracy by abolishing the life tenure system, and allowing modest electoral competition for the Party's Central Committee membership. However, Deng's political reform only achieved limited results, and his program of separating the Party from the government was discarded in 1989. Despite Deng's effort to promote younger, more educated, and more competent officials to Party leadership, intra-party politics throughout the 1980s and the early 1990s was overshadowed by oligarchy and septuagenarian/octogenarian rule. During the Jiang era, the Chinese elite has been preoccupied with developing the market economy, strengthening the legal system, and reducing the size of the government, while ignoring more significant political reform. Lack of democracy has contributed to widespread official corruption and increasing tension between government officials and ordinary people. As both Chinese society and the Party have become more diversified, the Party elite now apparently seeks to develop "intra-party democracy" through strengthening existent institutions of Party committees and congresses, and developing check-and-balance mechanisms and limited electoral competition within the Party.

Party Committees Strengthened

One of the likely institutional innovations regarding intra-Party democracy is to strengthen the function of Party committees at all levels. According to the Party constitution, the Central Committee of the CCP is defined, together with the National Party Congress, as the Party's highest leadership bodies. Local Party committees from the province (including four municipalities and five ethnic minority autonomous regions) to the county level, elected by Party congresses in their domains, are expected to be responsible to Party congresses at the same level and make policies according to instructions given by Party committees at a higher level. Since Party congresses at all levels have convened only once every five years, the Central Committee and local Party committees have normatively been considered as policymaking organs. Empirically, however, decisions are made in even smaller circles. At the central level, the real decision is made by the Politburo, particularly its standing committee headed by the core leader.[23] While the Central Committee may work as a formal "selectorate" to choose Party leaders or as a bargaining arena for policy debate, it often gives way to informal politics in leadership succession and merely ratifies policies made by the top leadership.[24] Similarly, standing committee members (*changwei*) of Party committees at the local level, especially Party secretaries, actually control the policymaking process within their domains.

To strengthen the function of Party committees at the various levels, the Party has adopted a norm of combining collective leadership with individual responsibility (*geren fengong fuze*) among members of Party committees. Collective leadership means that all members in Party committees should be equal in making policies regarding important issues (*zhongda wenti*). These issues should be fully discussed among committee members and followed by a free vote, and the final decision should be made based on the majority rule. Individual responsibility requires division of labor among Party committee members for implementing policies and handling day-to-day routine work. The following points are made clear:

- Party committees should make a distinction between important issues and routine work.
- No one in Party committees has the final say or veto power on important issues, which should be decided based on the principle of one member, one vote. The Party secretary serves as chair, organizer, and coordinator for the committee, taking responsibility for its routine work.
- The Party secretary and other members in the same committee should be equal. The Party secretary's power should be checked and overseen by other committee members.
- Meeting regulations and operational procedures within Party committees should be established and implemented effectively.[25]

Most of these arguments are not new. The CCP constitution stipulates that Party committees at all levels should collectively make decision on important issues, combining collective leadership with individual responsibility. Both Mao Zedong and Deng Xiaoping have emphasized that the first secretary of any Party committee should not have a final say on important policy issues, which should be decided by all committee members according to the principle of democratic centralism (*minzhu jizhongzhi*).[26] Nevertheless, both Mao and Deng ended up as patriarchal leaders who dominated Chinese politics for a half-century, because they failed to institutionalize Party committees as policymaking organs by developing sufficient meeting regulations and operational procedures. The best example is the Central Committee, which is expected to be a top policymaking organ but has functioned only symbolically throughout the history of the People's Republic of China (PRC).

As seen in Table 2.1, the Central Committee convened very irregularly during the Mao era. After the establishment of the PRC in 1949, the Central Committee convened only five plenums prior to the 8th National Congress in 1956, less than once a year on average. It assembled more often during the latter part of the 1950s (eight plenums in four years), but convened even more rarely after the early 1960s (eight plenums in sixteen years); with meeting periods for each plenum varying from as short as one day to as long as over one month! In the post-Mao era, the Central Committee convened more routinely (one to two times yearly, except for 1984 when no plenum was assembled), with each plenum lasting variously from one day to one week. The number of Central Committee members (excluding alternate members) has increased over the years, from 97 in 1956 to 198 in 2002. The main agenda items of these plenums are to elect—or, to be more precise, endorse the appointment of—Party leadership, including the Politburo and its standing committee, as well as the chairmanship (prior to 1982) or general secretaryship, and pass formal resolutions on important policy issues.

Institutionally, the Central Committee cannot function as a true decision-making organ given its infrequent meeting times. Apparently, Chinese reformers have acknowledged this problem and are considering increasing meeting time periods of the Central Committee.[27] Probably as the first step, the Party has chosen Shanghai as a trial spot where the municipal Party committee convenes its plenums three times yearly. In this case, it is emphasized that all important policies, cadre appointments or recalls, and projects, as well as the appropriation of major financing for large-scale capital projects (*sanzhong yida*) should be collectively decided by all members of the Shanghai Municipal Party Committee, rather than determined by the committee's "standing members" (*changwei*) or secretaries.[28] If this experiment goes well, the Central Committee may have more meeting sessions in the future for deciding important nationwide policy issues.

Reform on meeting regulations of the Central Committee has certain implications for the committee's membership structure. If the Central Committee is to become an influential policymaking body and meet more frequently, it will need more full-time members. However, most of the Central Committee members elected at the Party's 16th Congress are still scattered nationwide, serving as local Party or government leaders. This

Table 2.1. *Central Committee Plenums since the 8th CCP National Congress*

Year	Month/date	Meeting	Attendees[a]	Main agenda
1956	9/15–9/27	8th PC	1026	Revising Party constitution; passing 2nd 5-year plan; electing CC
1956	9/28	1st CC	170 (97)	Electing Politburo, SC, and CC chairmanships
1956	11/10–11/15	2nd CC		Domestic economic and international issues
1957	9/20–10/9	3rd CC		Party rectification; 12-year agriculture program
1958	5/3	4th CC		Discussing Political Report to 2nd Assembly of 8th PC
1958	5/5–5/23	Assembly		Approving general line of socialist construction
1958	5/25	5th CC		Electing Lin Piao vice chairman, adding others to Politburo
1958	11/28–12/10	6th CC		People's Commune; Mao not candidate for PRC president
1959	4/2–4/5	7th CC		Economic work; preparing for 2nd NPC
1959	7/2–8/16	8th CC		On Ten Relations; Peng Dehuai case
1961	1/14–1/18	9th CC		Economic adjustment; People's Commune
1962	9/24–9/27	10th CC		Economic adjustment; rural economy
1966	8/1–8/12	11th CC		On Cultural Revolution
1968	10/13–10/31	12th CC		Liu Shaoqi officially purged; preparing for 9th PC
1969	4/1–4/24	9th PC	1512	Revising Party constitution; electing CC
1969	4/28	1st CC	279 (170)	Electing Politburo, SC, and CC chairmanships
1970	8/23–9/6	2nd CC		Economic Plan for 1970; preparing for 4th NPC
1973	8/24–8/28	10th PC	1249	Revising Party constitution; electing CC
1973	8/30	1st CC	319 (195)	Electing Politburo, SC, and CC chairmanships
1975	1/8–1/10	2nd CC		Preparing for 4th NPC; Deng as Party vice chairman again
1977	7/16–7/21	3rd CC		Gang of Four officially purged; preparing for 11th PC
1977	8/12–8/18	11th PC	1510	Revising Party constitution; electing CC
1977	8/19	1st CC	333 (201)	Electing Politburo, SC, and CC chairmanships
1978	2/18–2/23	2nd CC		Preparing for 5th NPC and CPPCC
1978	12/18–12/22	3rd CC		Economic construction as priority; "two whatever" criticized
1979	9/25–9/28	4th CC		On agricultural development
1980	2/23–2/29	5th CC		Party constitution, Secretariat reinstated, Liu Shaoqi rehabilitated
1981	6/27–6/29	6th CC		On Party history since 1949; Hu and Zhao added to leadership
1982	8/6	7th CC		Political Report to 12th PC; Party constitution revision resolution

Table 2.1. *Central Committee Plenums since the 8th CCP National Congress (continued)*

Year	Month/date	Meeting	Attendees[a]	Main agenda
1982	9/1–9/11	12th PC	1545	Revising Party constitution; electing CC, CAC, CDIC
1982	9/12–9/13	1st CC	348 (210)	Electing Politburo, SC, and general secretary; deciding CMC leadership
1983	10/11–10/12	2nd CC		Party consolidation; preparing for 6th NPC and CPPCC
1983	10/20	3rd CC		Economic system reform, deciding to convene Party assembly
1985	9/16	4th CC		Party rejuvenation; 7th 5-year plan; to convene Party Assembly
1985	9/18–9/23	Assembly		Electing new members to CC; electing CAC and CDIC
1985	9/24	5th CC		Party rejuvenation; new leaders added to Politburo
1986	9/28	6th CC		On socialist civilization
1987	10/20	7th CC		Political Report to 13th PC; Party constitution revision resolution
1987	10/25–11/1	13th PC	1,936	Revising Party constitution; electing CC, CAC, CDIC
1987	11/2	1st CC	285 (175)	Electing Politburo, SC, and CMC general secretary; deciding CMC leadership; approving CAC and CDIC leaders
1988	3/15–3/19	2nd CC		Prepare for 7th NPC and CPPCC
1988	9/26–9/30	3rd CC		On price and wage reform and other economic issues
1989	6/23–6/24	4th CC		Leadership adjusted
1989	11/6–11/9	5th CC		On economic consolidation; Deng resigned, electing new CMC
1990	3/9–3/12	6th CC		Enhancing Party–mass relations
1990	12/25–12/30	7th CC		Ten-year program and 8th 5-year plan
1991	11/25–11/29	8th CC		Agricultural work; deciding to convene 14th PC
1992	10/5–9/1992	9th CC		Political Report to 14th PC; Party constitution revision resolution
1992	10/12–10/18	14th PC	2,000	Revising Party constitution; electing CC, CDIC
1992	10/19	1st CC	319 (189)	Electing Politburo, SC, and CMC general secretary; deciding CMC leadership; approving CDIC leaders
1993	3/5–3/7	2nd CC		Preparing for 8th NPC and CPPCC; Party/government structure reform
1993	11/11–11/14	3rd CC		Establishing the socialist market economy
1994	9/25–9/28	4th CC		Party building, adding Huang Ju to Politburo

Table 2.1. *Central Committee Plenums since the 8th CCP National Congress (continued)*

Year	Month/date	Meeting	Attendees[a]	Main agenda
1995	9/25–9/28	5th CC		Ninth 5-year plan; CMC personnel change; Chen Xitong case
1996	10/7–10/10	6th CC		Socialist civilization
1997	9/6–9/9	7th CC		Political Report to 15th PC; Party constitution revision resolution
1997	9/12–9/18	15th PC	2074	Revising Party constitution; electing CC and CDIC
1997	9/19	1st CC	344 (193)	Electing Politburo, SC, and general secretary; deciding CMC leadership; approving CDIC leaders
1998	2/25–2/26	2nd CC		Preparing for 9th NPC and CPPCC, State Council structure reform
1998	10/12–10/14	3rd CC		Agricultural work
1999	9/19–9/22	4th CC		SOE reform; promoting Hu Jintao to CMC
2000	10/9–10/11	5th CC		Tenth 5-year plan
2001	9/24–9/26	6th CC		Party style construction
2002	11/3–11/5	7th CC		Political Report to 16th PC; Party constitution revision resolution
2002	11/8–11/14	16th PC	2120	Revising Party constitution; electing CC and CDIC
2002	11/15	1st CC	356 (198)	Electing Politburo, SC, and CMC general secretary; deciding CMC leadership; approving CDIC leaders

[a] Number of full members of the Central Committee in parentheses.
CAC, Party's Central Advisor Commission; CC, Central Committee of the CCP; CDIC, Central Discipline Inspection Commission; CMC, CCP Central Military Commission; CPPCC, Chinese People's Political Consultative Conference; NPC, National People's Congress; PC, National Party Congress; SC, Politburo's standing committee.

membership structure does not suggest that the Central Committee will improve its function significantly in the foreseeable future. Even the new Politburo, with twenty-four members, cannot be perceived as an ultimate decision-making organ. Because only a number of provincial Party secretaries took a seat in the Politburo, it cannot legitimately claim to be an institution representing assorted interests of various provinces. The even number of its membership also suggests that the Politburo is unlikely to make decisions on controversial issues through majority votes, unless a clear majority (two-thirds of total votes)—rather than a simple majority—is required in policymaking within the Politburo.[29] In contrast, the nine-member standing committee of the Politburo, which excludes local leaders, remains the highest decision-making organ. Despite Beijing's declaration to improve the rules of procedure and decision-making mechanisms within Party committees and to give fuller play to the role of plenary sessions of the committees,[30] Party committees are less likely to be strengthened significantly at the central level than the local level.

Party Congresses Empowered

Another likely institutional innovation is to improve the system of Party congresses, a goal first set up at the 15th National Party Congress in 1997. As one Chinese scholar has proposed, the Party should follow the regulation made at its 8th National Party Congress (1956) mandating Party congresses at all levels to convene once a year (*lianhuizhi*).[31] This idea is fully developed in a book entitled *A Great Platform for Party Building in the New Century—Instruction to Studying General Secretary Jiang Zemin's July 1 Speech*, co-authored by theorists and professors in the Central Party School. Some of the book's main arguments are as follows:

- Improving Party congress system is fundamental to developing democratic centralism within the Party. The Party congress system should be as essential to the Party as the National People's Congress (NPC) system is to the state.
- At any given level, Party congresses are the most important bodies, with power to decide crucial issues (*zhongda shiwu*) and supervise other Party organizations.
- Party congresses should convene annual meetings, just as the NPC has done.
- Meeting regulations and operation procedures must be improved to ensure good discussion at Party congresses.
- Party committees should make policies according to resolutions made by Party congresses at the same level, and upon instructions given by Party committees at a higher level.[32]

These viewpoints from inside the prestigious Central Party School look more like policy proposals than mere academic discussion. As a matter of fact, by the end of 2001 the Party's Organization Department had selected ten counties nationwide as trial spots where Party congresses convene annually rather than once every five years.[33] In summer 2002, China's official media outlet, the New Chinese News Agency, published an article on Party constitution revision. The article argues that the organization system of the Party consists of two basic institutions—congresses and committees at all levels—but Party history has been inconsistent as to whether congresses should convene once every five years (*dingqizhi*) or once a year.[34] Mention of such institutional flexibility in an article related to Party constitution revision prior to the 16th National Party Congress suggests that some people within the Party intended to empower Party congresses by convening annual meetings. In the following months, other influential scholars in the Central Party School endorsed the idea of having annual meetings for Party congresses.[35]

Another perspective on strengthening the functions of Party congresses is to turn them into real "electoral colleges" for electing Party committees at different levels. Starting from a theoretical distinction between normative democracy and empirical democracy, some scholars argue that the key feature of democracy is to elect political leaders through just competition and full participation. With this approach, they believe that the main function of Party congresses is to elect Party committees. The priority on strengthening Party congresses, therefore, is to improve their electoral functions by providing more candidates than positions to Party congress delegates, so that they can have free choice in electing Party committee members. According to this perspective, should Party congresses convene annually and become real policymaking organs, it would significantly increase meeting costs and reduce the Party's work efficiency.[36] In other words, Party congresses should be redefined as (effectively) electoral colleges, rather than the supreme power organ of the Party.

China's new leaders are apparently attempting to improve the function of Party congresses and committees from the bottom up, as Jiang Zemin indicated in his report to the 16th National Party Congress:

> We should establish and improve an intra-party democratic system that fully reflects the will of Party members and organizations, starting with the reform of the relevant systems and mechanisms on the basis of guaranteeing the democratic rights of Party members and giving priority to improving the systems of Party congresses and of Party committees. The system of Party congresses with regular annual meetings should be tried out in more cities and counties. We should explore ways to give play to the role of delegates when Party congresses are not in session.[37]

The strengthening of the Party congress system may provide a new channel for delegates to the congresses at the central and local levels to participate in Party affairs, thus expanding the power base shared by the Party elite. At the central level, if the National Party Congress, an "electoral college" for selecting the Central Committee and a "rubber stamp" for endorsing Party constitution revision, is to transform itself into the "highest decision-making organ" in the future, it may provide a constant institutional forum for the Party delegates to meet once a year, subjecting the Central Committee to the supervision of the National Party Congress periodically. At the local level, with the experimental practice of holding county and municipal Party congresses annually, congressional delegates are likely to play an intermediate role between Party members and Party committees, thus making Party committees more or less responsible to Party members.

Checks and Balances within the Party

Institutionally, the strengthening of Party congresses and Party committees from the central to the county level will inevitably involve a new division of power between these two sets of Party organization. Historically, the Party's ruling system was designed according to the Marxist-Leninist principle of "combining legislative and executive into one organ" (*yixing heyi*) to ensure concentration of power and political efficiency. Like Marx and Lenin, the Chinese Communists denigrated the liberal principle of separation of powers from the very beginning. Following the Leninist principle of democratic centralism and the Soviet political model, the Chinese Communists have, theoretically, still regarded the National Party Congress as the Party's highest power organ. Because the National Party Congress seldom assembles, the Central Committee is defined as the highest power organ when the National Party Congress is in adjournment. As a result, the Central Party Committee as well as Party committees at local levels theoretically enjoy three kinds of power—policymaking, policy implementation, and Party discipline inspection—within their jurisdictions. As discussed above, the real power is actually concentrated in the hands of the Politburo's standing committee and "standing members" of local Party committees.

If Party congresses are to be strengthened by convening annual meetings, what will be the new role for Party committees—the standing bodies of Party congresses? Will Party committees become more important policymaking organs, or less important? Will that make Party discipline inspection commissions (DICs) independent organs responsible to Party congresses, rather than to Party committees in the future? One proponent for establishing check-and-balance mechanisms within the Party has published an article related to these issue in an influential journal *Zhongguo Dangzheng Ganbu Luntan* (Chinese Cadre Forum), which was republished in *Cankao Wenxue* (Selected Works for Reference) in early 2002. The article's main arguments are as follows:

- To dilute the power of Party committees (*dangweihui*) by delineating them as responsible for policymaking only, run by the principle of democratic centralism (collective decision-making). Party committees at the county, municipal, or provincial levels should consist of various numbers of regular members (30 for each county committee, 40 for each municipal committee, and 50 for each provincial committee) and standing committee members (9 for a county, 11 for a municipality, and 13 for a province). Among these members, 40 percent should be senior Party cadres who have no positions within executive committees, DICs, or government and judicial organs; 40 percent should be ordinary Party members in all walks of life; and 20 percent are experts on Party building.
- To create executive committees (*zhiweihui*) as responsible for implementing Party policies, managed by the leading cadre (*shouzhang fuzezhi*) for the sake of efficiency. Membership of executive committees would vary at the county, municipal, and provincial levels (five for a county, seven for a municipality, and nine for a province). Executive committees would nominate Party department heads within respective domains, pending approval of Party committees at the same level. Party cadres lower than department heads could be appointed or recalled by executive committees.
- To increase the authority of DICs (*jiweihui*) in watching executive committees. Members of DICs could attend and speak at executive committee meetings, review documents issued by executive committees, and inspect and oversee policy implementation on the part of executive committees, investigate and punish cadres nominated or appointed by executive committees in cases of Party discipline violation. The DIC personnel should be appointed vertically, free of control of local Party committees and executive committees.
- To make a division of power among Party committees, executive committees, and DICs. The three organizations, without overlapping personnel, are all responsible to Party congresses at the same level.

During congressional adjournment periods, Party committees lead executive committees and DICs.

• Delegates to Party congresses should have a right to inquire and criticize members of Party committees, executive committees, and DICs during annual meetings. A motion to recall unqualified leader cadres in the Party can be initiated by five or more delegates and then decided by congresses. During congressional adjournment periods, delegates can collect opinions and suggestions from Party members and ordinary people within their constituencies.[38]

This proposal only intends to develop check-and-balance mechanisms within the Party at the local level. Reportedly, a similar proposal prepared by the Policy Research Office of the Central Discipline Inspection Commission has been submitted to the secretariat of the CCP Central Committee. According to this proposal, Party congresses at the local level should convene once a year. Party congresses and their standing bodies would be responsible for policymaking (*juece*); Party committees would take care of policy implementation (*zhixing*); and DICs would serve as independent bodies for discipline supervision (*jiandu*).[39] One difference between these two proposals is whether Party committees should be treated as standing bodies of Party congresses (as they have always been), or be redefined as executive committees for policy implementation.

It is unclear whether China's new Party leadership will put this spectacular proposal in its reform agenda. In view of the Party's experiment with the reform of the Party committee system, a more likely scenario is that plenary sessions of Party committees will become major venues for collective decision making, while standing members of Party committees will be responsible for policy implementation. In other words, a division of power might occur within a local Party committee, but not between two parallel local Party organizations.

Introducing Electoral Competition into the Party

Electoral competition was absent during the Mao era. It was not until the early 1980s that the reform elite under Deng began to allow limited electoral competition within the Party. At the 12th Party Congress in 1982, delegates for the first time were allowed to add names to, and delete names from, the list of nominees for the Central Committee provided by the leadership.[40] At the 13th Party Congress in 1987, the election rules for the Cen-

tral Committee were further reformed to require more nominees than the
number of seats (*cha' e xuanju*). With the reform, the number of candidates for membership in the Central Committee must exceed the number
of slots by 5 percent.[41] The marginal difference in number between candidates and seats, plus the Party's control of the nomination process, has significantly limited the voters' free choice and veto power, but it nevertheless prevents the most disliked nominees from being elected to the Party
Congress or the Central Committee, as happened at the 15th National Party
Congress in 1997. However, such an arrangement of more candidates than
positions has been irrelevant to the formation of the Party's higher power
organ, the Politburo (as well as its standing committee).[42] As the numbers
of candidates for the Politburo and its standing committee are equal to the
numbers of positions available, Central Committee members tend to simply endorse the Party's nominees during the plenums. Any possible disputes over the formation of the Politburo are precluded through deliberation and negotiation among Central Committee members prior to the
electoral ceremony to ensure their unanimous endorsement of leadership
decision. As noted in Chapter 1, prior to the 16th Party Congress, reformers in the Party had lobbied for a larger "margin of elimination" (*cha'e*)
when congressional delegates elect Central Committee members, and for
some margin of elimination when the latter elect members of the Politburo.
Unfortunately, "margin of elimination" for electing Central Committee at
the 16th Party Congress remained 5 percent, and no "margin of elimination" was ever applied to elect the Politburo as well as its standing committee. In selecting the candidates for the new Central Committee, the
Party went through the following steps prior to the 16th National Party
Congress, starting in May 2001.

- The Party leadership sent forty-six investigation teams (plus five
  teams sent by the Central Military Commission) to various departments, thirty-one provinces (including municipalities and ethnic minority autonomous regions), and twenty-three key state enterprises to
  pick up preliminary candidates. A total of 32,200 Party heads at the
  county level and above were involved in recommending possible
  candidates to the investigation teams (although at the central leaders'
  instruction, the investigation teams might have had some predeter-
  mined candidates in mind before going to local areas).
- The investigation teams selected 514 candidates as potential full or
  alternate members of the Central Committee, followed by individual

consultation between team members and 19,200 Party heads regarding personal credentials and work performance of the 514 candidates. During March 2002, the investigation teams selected 462 candidates out of the original list of 514.

- In October 2002, the Politburo's Standing Committee selected about 375 candidates out of the list submitted by the investigation teams. This smaller list was approved by the Politburo and submitted to the congressional delegates for discussion.
- Delegates, who were grouped in 38 delegations, first elected 356 candidates (198 candidates for full members, and 158 for alternate members) out of the list of 375. A modest margin of elimination was applied at this stage. Out of 208 candidates for Central Committee membership, 198 were elected, with an elimination margin of 10 (5.1 percent). Out of 167 candidates for alternate members, 158 were elected, with an elimination margin of 9 (5.7 percent).
- Delegates as a whole formally elected the Central Committee on November 14, 2002. All candidates preliminarily elected by the 38 delegations respectively were elected into the Central Committee. Central Committee members were listed according the strokes of their names written in Chinese (starting with the name with the simplest strokes), while alternate members were listed according to the number of votes they received from the delegations.[43]

The above procedures clearly demonstrate that in (s)electing the Central Committee, modest competition was overshadowed by the appointment of candidates from top down. While several rounds of deliberation and consultation were taken before the final candidates were selected, most Party members were not involved in the process at all. Furthermore, delegates to the 16th National Party Congress, theoretically elected by all Party members, had little choice in electing the Central Committee members, because the margin of elimination was too small.

Electoral competition for Party positions is more significant at the grassroots level, where the Party's village branches in some regions have experimented with the two-ballot system since 1992. According to this system initiated in Hequ County, Shanxi Province, the secretary and all members of the village Party branch are subject to a two-stage election. At the first stage, the incumbent secretary presents a report to villagers' representatives and answers their questions, and villagers' representatives then recommend candidates for the positions of Party secretary and other branch members by casting a secret ballot. Party members receiving over 50 percent of the ballots will become preliminary candidates from which township Party Committee nominates official candidates for the Party branch. At the second stage, the village Party members elect the secretary and other Party branch members.[44] The significance of the two-ballot system is to prevent those most disliked from being elected, but the system cannot guarantee that those elected are the most liked by the Party members or the ordinary villagers, since official candidates are determined by the township Party committee. The rationale that non-Party members should have a voice in the first-stage of the Party branch election is that the Party secretary in China's grassroots often manages the affairs of the whole village, not merely those of the Party. Since the village Party branch, rather than the elected village committee, has the final say in many villages, the two-ballot system can be justified for the sake of village self-governance. In general, it may enhance the legitimacy of the village Party branch as the core of leadership in China's grassroots.

Implications for Democratizing the Whole Society

A rising tide of interest in developing intra-party democracy is apparent among Chinese liberals' academic discourse. Some Chinese intellectuals hope to promote democracy in the society (*shehui minzhu*) through developing intra-party democracy, believing that the CCP is both leader and promoter of China's political reform.[45] Such strategic thinking is supported by an assumption that the Party is an indispensable force for maintaining political order in China. The 16th National Party Congress endorsed this way of thinking by declaring that "intra-party democracy is the life of the Party and plays an important exemplary and leading role in people's democracy."[46] Even so, developing intra-party democracy, ironically, may have negative implications for China's process toward full democratization in the short term, enhancing the ruling Party's legitimacy and reducing civil society's demands for multiparty democracy and electoral competition among different parties.

Increasing Party Penetration in Society

As indicated previously, with the "Three Represents" being enshrined in the Party constitution, more intellectual and economic elites are likely to be recruited into the Party, particularly private entrepreneurs and free-lance intellectuals who are not part of the working class. As the Party has become a more diverse and elitist-oriented organization, its traditional ruling methods are facing new challenges. In the Mao era, the revolutionary elite could easily reach the goal of democratic centralism among Party members—representatives of the proletariat—through ideological indoctrination, political campaigns, and patriarchal leadership. Such a style has lost its relevance because of the changing Party membership. The reform elite within the Party has apparently realized the necessity of improving the "representation mechanism" (*daibiao jizhi*), which is aimed at ensuring that the Party can represent the diversified interests of the overwhelming majority of the Chinese people. Establishing such a mechanism would require a close and positive interaction being developed between the "Represents" and the represented, so that the represented can supervise in a timely and effective manner the "Represents" in public affairs.[47] Some argue that the National Party Congress, based on the principle of representative democracy, should be the final decision maker in Party affairs.[48]

While the recruitment of social elites into the Party has provided new incentives for developing intra-Party democracy, it may also undermine the growth of an independent civil society free of the Party's control and reduce social pressure for establishing multiparty democracy in China. Theoretically, an autonomous bourgeoisie and a "modern dynamic plural-ist society" are widely accepted as crucial conditions for liberal democracy.[49] China's incomplete market and property rights reforms, however, have not yet created an independent middle class. In addition to intimate connections between government officials and entrepreneurs (state or private) that have contributed to widely spread corruption, many Chinese intellectuals see Party membership as a necessary tool to reach their career goals. They believe that China, under its current regime, stands a reasonable chance of successfully completing its economic and political transitions with peace and stability.[50] They also believe that the best way to reform the Party, as political dissident Fang Lizhi and intellectual Liu Ji coincidently advocated in the 1980s, is to join the Party.[51] The publication of *Yu Zongshuji Tanxin* (Talking with the General Secretary), a book compiled by fourteen young scholars in Beijing's Chinese Academy of Social Sciences (CASS) and supported by Liu Ji (former vice president of CASS and advisor to Jiang Zemin), illustrated well the *mutual penetration* between the Party and intellectuals in recent years.[52] Consequently, the opposition movement and social protests after 1989 only occurred sporadically and at a small scale without strong support from an independent middle class. The recruitment of private entrepreneurs into the Party is likely to win over their political support for the regime, by expanding Party membership in private enterprises, a political vacuum created by China's property rights reform. It is unclear whether the Party's bid to co-opt businesspeople will ensure its continued dominance in Chinese society.[53] For the time being, however, such a preemptive strategy may serve to thwart potential demands from the private sector for radical political reform and multiparty democracy in China.

"Anchoring Party Leadership to the Government"

While the goal of Chinese reformers is to maintain the legitimate rule of the CCP, their strategies vary over time. During the 1980s, reformers led by Deng Xiaoping attempted to develop socialist democracy through "separating the Party from the government" (*dangzheng fenkai*). According to Deng's blueprint, Party leaders at all levels should be prohibited from concurrently holding government positions.[54] As Deng elaborated:

> The Party's main functions are to work out its own guidelines and state policies, exercising overall leadership. Through legal processes, the organs of state power convert the Party's political line into state intentions and are responsible for this implementation and administration.[55]

Deng's idea of "separating the Party from the government" was practiced before and after the 13th Party Congress in 1987, but has been rarely mentioned since 1990. Despite Deng's effort to separate the Party's role from that government, it is in fact difficult to draw a fine line between the two institutions in a one-party system. Functional ambiguity between the Party and government created power conflicts between the Party general secretary and the premier throughout the 1980s.

Deng's idea of power division was replaced by a new formula of "anchoring Party leadership to the government" (*yudang yuzheng*, or *jiandang yuzheng*) during the Jiang era.[56] At the 8th NPC in 1993, Party General Secretary Jiang Zemin assumed the post of the PRC president, serving as "core leader." Around him, another two top leaders, Li Peng and Qiao Shi, also concurrently served as premier and NPC chairman, respectively. The 9th NPC followed this unwritten norm, with Jiang retaining the presidency, Li obtaining the NPC chairmanship, and Zhu Rongji taking the premiership. After the 16th CCP Congress, Jiang's designated successor Hu Jintao took both the secretaryship and presidency from Jiang.

This 1993 institutional innovation is actually a restoration of an early practice in PRC history, which recognizes government departments as *indispensable arenas for policy formulation*. After establishment of the PRC, Party Chairman Mao Zedong concurrently served as head of state from 1949 to 1959. Party Vice Chairman Liu Shaoqi served as NPC chairman between 1954 and 1959, and another Party vice chairman, Zhou Enlai, retained the premiership of the State Council until he died in 1976. After Liu Shaoqi assumed the office of state president in 1959, Mao maintained his Party chairmanship and remained the paramount leader on the "second front," while Liu took care of day-to-day state affairs on the "first front"—an institutional design and precedent that probably inspired Deng's reform blueprint of Party–government separation. However, the uneasy relationship between Mao and Liu ended up with Liu's dismissal as president and the abolition of the state presidential office during the Cultural Revolution, a period when government offices were overwhelmingly replaced by "revolutionary committees" or "Party core groups" (*dang de hexin xiaozu*) in the name of enhancing the Party's unitary leadership (*yiyuanhua lingdao*).

Retrospectively, periods in which "anchoring Party leadership to the government" was practiced—the 1950s and the 1990s—were notable for the relative lack of political tension. Thus, from the perspective of "path dependency," which emphasizes the impact of past choice on current institutions, the Chinese elite is likely to formalize this informal norm in the post-Jiang era. No signs in the Chinese media and official speeches in the wake of the 16th Party Congress have suggested that Beijing is going to resurrect the norm of "separating the Party from the government." While the Party in the 1980s attempted to retreat from governmental affairs to a certain degree, it now intends to enhance its control of state affairs through directly placing supreme Party leaders in top government positions. Without a multiparty system allowing for electoral competition for government positions, the problems of Party dominance over government and the overlapping of Party and government functions cannot be really resolved. Domesticating the ruling Party (with revolutionary legacy) to routinized state affairs may make it even more difficult for the state to gain its autonomy from the Party's continuing control in the immediate future.

Conclusion

The "Three Represents" idea reflects the CCP's new efforts to reconcile its traditional doctrine with an increasingly diverse society. It suggests that the Party has abandoned its ideological preference for state enterprises and redefined itself as the vanguard of the Chinese people. By so doing, the Party attempts to expand its ruling base and establish a tripod pyramid consisting of political, economic, and intellectual elites. It also adopts an open mind toward different political civilizations, realizing the necessity of coexistence and mutual learning among various social systems in the world.

There are no signs that China's new leadership is going to change the one-party ruling system in the foreseeable future. Rather, Beijing's major goal is to perpetuate the CCP's ruling legitimacy through developing intra-party democracy. Possible measures include: (1) making Party committees of all levels more effective by implementing collective leadership and majority rule among committee members; (2) expanding the power base of the Party elite by strengthening Party congresses; (3) developing check-and-balance mechanisms within the Party; and (4) increasing intra-party electoral competition.

It is uncertain whether Beijing can reach the goal of developing intra-party democracy without *concomitant* democratization of the whole society. Even if the new measures make the Party leadership more responsible to its members, they do not render it accountable to society as a whole. In the absence of meaningful restraints on the Party's monopoly of power and the consequent blurring of lines between Party and state authority, it has proved impossible "for the National People's Congress to pass laws independently of Party initiative, for courts to act autonomously, or for the mass media to scrutinize critically the behavior of top officials."[57]

In past decades, the Chinese reform elite has adopted a cost-saving, shock-reducing strategy by developing new institutions from inside the old system. Political reform has therefore followed a gradualist trajectory with theoretical inconsistency and strategic ambiguity, without a concrete alternative paradigm to the present political system. The official ideology remains influential in Chinese politics, although its main function has been changed from offensively transforming people's ideas to defensively maintaining the ruling Party's legitimacy in a changing society. Administrative reform and the marginal power division within the government are cautiously implemented without threatening the Party's monopoly on political power. Electoral competition is allowed at the village level or other areas, but is not relevant to more significant Party and government positions. In spite of Beijing's efforts at promoting the rule of law, it also endorses the notion of the rule by virtue or rule by law under the Party's leadership. As Kent Jennings observed some years ago, the existence of powerful Party organs, the thorough penetration of society by the state, the scarcity of independent advocacy groups, a shackled mass media, and the absence of free and competitive elections had supplied a unique meaning to Chinese-style democracy.[58] These phenomena are likely to continue in the early post-Jiang era, given the Party's priorities and strategies regarding political reform, as well as China's incomplete property rights reform and immature civil society, as discussed in the following chapters.

Notes

1. Li Junru, "Zhonggong Fen Sanjieduan Zhunbei Shiliuda Lilun" [The CCP Has Prepared the Theory for the 16th National Congress through Three Stages], *Outlook* (Beijing), August 12, 2002.

2. For a full discussion of the characteristics of the Chinese regime, see Gang Lin, "China's Democratic Prospect in the Post-Deng Era," in *Transition towards Post-Deng China*, ed. Xiaobo Hu and Gang Lin (Singapore: Singapore University Press, 2001), 253–255.

3. Jiang Zemin, speech at the Central Party School, May 31, 2002, New Chinese News Agency, available at www.xinhuanet.com, accessed on June 1, 2002.

4. Elisabeth Rosenthal, "China's Communists Try to Decide What They Stand For," *New York Times*, May 1, 2002.

5. Ye Weishi, "Sange Daibiao Zhongyao Sixiang Xingcheng he Fazhang Mailuo" [The Formation and Development of the Important Thought of "Three Represents"], *Jiefang Ribao*, July 2, 2002.

6. Jiang Zemin, "Speech at the 80th Anniversary of the Founding of the CCP," *People's Daily*, July 1, 2001; Jiang Zemin, "Report to the 16th National Party Congress," *New Chinese News Agency*, available at www.xinhuanet.com, accessed on November 8, 2002.

7. Borrowed from Marxist theory of political economy, the term productive forces refers to laborers and means of production, and the productive relations refer to ownership of productive means, human relations during production, and the product distribution system.

8. Susan L. Shirk, *The Political Logic of Economic Reform in China* (Berkeley: University of California Press, 1993), 23.

9. Ma Licheng and Ling Zhijun, *Jiaofeng* [Confrontation] (Beijing: Jinri Zhongguo Chubanshe, 1998), 242–267.

10. As Deng Xiaoping specified, reaching the goal of communism in China required long-term efforts by several dozen generations (*jishidai*), presumably ranging between 20 generations to 99 generations. If we count a generation as 20 years, this long period could be 400 years at least and 1,980 years at most. When Deng was asked whether he

had actually meant several generations, Deng confirmed that what he meant was *jishidai.*

11. Jiang, "Report to the 16th National Party Congress."

12. Wang Changjiang et al., *Xinshiji Dang de Jianshe de Weida Gangling—Xuexi Jiang Zemin Zongshuji Qiyi Jianghua Fudao* [Great Platform for Party Building in the New Century—Instruction to Studying General Secretary Jiang Zemin's July 1 Speech] (Beijing: Zhongyang Dangxiao Chubanshe, 2001), 48.

13. Anonymous Party official, interview by author, Beijing, June 3, 2000; Susan V. Lawrence, "Three Cheers for the Party," *Far Eastern Economic Review*, October 26, 2000.

14. Jiang, "Speech at the 80th Anniversary of the Founding of the CCP."

15. John Pomfret and Philip P. Pan, "China's Leader Opens Party to the Country's New Rich," *Washington Post*, November 8, 2002, A21; Susan V. Lawrence, "Jiang Ensures Party Endures," *Far Eastern Economic Review*, November 21, 2002, 34–38.

16. Ye, "Sange Daibiao Zhongyao Sixiang Xingcheng he Fazhang Mailuo."

17. Xie Fangyi, "Zhengdang Xiandaihua: Zhizhengdang Mianlin de Yige Zhongda er Jinpo de Lilun yu Shijian Keti" [The Party's Modernization: An Important Theoretical and Practical Issue Facing the Ruling Party], *Tizhi Gaige* [System Reform], no. 9, 2001: 15. (Originally published in *Ziliao Tongxun* [Materials and Communication], July/August, 9–13, 2001.)

18. Wang Jingsong, *Zhonghua Renmin Gongheguo de Zhengfu he Zhengzhi* [The Government and Politics of the People's Republic of China] (Beijing: Zhongyang Dangxiao Chubanshe, 1994), 263.

19. Wan Bing and Xue Guangzhou, *Minzhu Zexue* [Philosophy of Democracy] (Zhejiang: Zhejiang Renmin Chubanshe, 1994), 152.

20. Dong Yuyu and Shi Binhai, eds., *Zhengzhi Zhongguo* [Chinese Politics] (Beijing: Jinri Zhongguo Chubanshe, 1998); Ma Licheng and Ling Zhijun, *Jiaofeng.*

21. Liu Junning, "The Intellectual Turn: The Emergence of Liberalism in Contemporary China," in *China's Future: Constructive Partner or Emerging Threat?* ed. Ted Galen Carpenter and James A. Dorn (Washington, D.C.: Cato Institute, 2000), 58.

22. Yang Deshan, "Developing Socialist Political Civilization," available at www.xinhuanet.com, accessed on September 6, 2002; "Remarks on Socialist Political Civilization by Experts and Scholars," available at www.xinhuanet.com, accessed on November 14, 2002.

23. Hu Wei, *Zhengfu Guocheng* [Process of Government] (Zhejiang: Zhejiang Renmin Chubanshe, 1998), 87–88.

24. Shirk, *The Political Logic of Economic Reform in China*, 90–91.

25. Wang et al., *Xinshiji Dang de Jianshe de Weida Gangling*, 131–134.

26. Mao Zedong, *Selected Works of Mao Zedong*, vol. 2 (Beijing: Renmin Chubanshe, 1986), 820–821; Deng Xiaoping, *Selected Works of Deng Xiaoping*, vol. 2 (Beijing: Renmin Chubanshe, 1993), 331, 341.

27. Jin Taijun, "Xinshiji Zhongguo Zhengzhi Gaige Ruogan Zhongda Wenti de Sikao" [Thought on Several Important Issues Regarding China's Political Reform in the New Century], *Zhongguo Zhengzhi* [Chinese Politics], no. 11 (2001): 29.

28. Anonymous Party official, Washington, D.C., December 2, 2001.

29. It is interesting to note that the numbers for members of Central Committee (198), Politburo (24), and the Politburo Standing Committee (9) are all divisible by three, thus making it easier to calculate two-thirds of the votes for the Central Commit-

tee (132), Politburo (16), and Politburo Standing Committee (6). The rule of a clear majority could be more acceptable than simple majority to the Party, given its traditional preference for consensus and unanimity in decision making. Although no sufficient evidence can be found to support such a speculation about the nontransparent policymaking process at the CCP's top level, one local Party committee does apply the clear majority rule for deciding cadre appointments in its domain. See *Tizhi Gaige* (Beijing), no. 1 (2001): 21–22.

30. Jiang, "Report to the 16th National Party Congress."

31. Jin, "Xinshiji Zhongguo Zhengzhi Gaige Ruogan Zhongda Wenti de Sikao," 30.

32. Wang et al., *Xinshiji Dang de Jianshe de Weida Gangling*, 126–130.

33. Li Yongzhong, "Guanyu Gaige Dangwei 'Yixing Heyi' Lingdao Tizhi de Sikao" [On Reforming the Ruling System of "Combining Executive and Legislative Functions into One Organ" within Party Committees], *Tizhi Gaige*, no. 4 (2002): 29.

34. Ye Duchu, "Zenyang Shi Dangzhang Chengwe Zengqiang Tuanjie, Xianshi Huoli, Youyuanze, Youxiwang de Wenjian" [How to Make the Party Constitution a Document that Increases Our Unity, Manifests Vitality, Is Principled, and Hopeful], July 26, 2002, available at www.xinhuanet.com, accessed on July 28, 2002.

35. "Ruling for the People and Party Building—Remarks by Zhang Zhiming," Strengthening China Forum, *People's Daily*, July 30, 2002, available at www.qglt.com, acccssscd on August 15, 2002; Liu Yantang, "Party Building over 13 Years—Interviewing with Lu Xianfu," Xinhuanet, September 24, 2002, available at www.xinhuanet.com, accessed on September 26, 2002; "On Party Congresses— Remarks by Xie Chuntao," Xinhuanet, November 6, 2002, available at www.xinhuanet.com, accessed on November 7, 2002.

36. Li Huairen, "Jianshe Shehuizhuyi Zhengzhi Wenming de Silu yu Tupokou" [Some Thought on the Starting Point for Developing Socialist Political Civilization], *Tizhi Gaige*, no. 7 (2002): 5.

37. Jiang, "Report to the 16th National Party Congress."

38. Li Yongzhong, "Guanyu Gaige Dangwei 'Yixing Heyi' Lingdao Tizhi de Sikao," 29–30.

39. "Zhonggong Yujiang Dangwei Quanli Yifenweisan" [The Chinese Communist Party Plans to Make a Division of Power among Three Branches within the Party Committee], *Xinwen Ziyou Daobao*, August 8, 2002.

40. James Wang, *Contemporary Chinese Politics: An Introduction* (Englewood Cliffs, N.J.: Prentice Hall, 1989), 81.

41. Minxin Pei, *From Reform to Revolution: The Demise of Communism in China and the Soviet Union* (Cambridge, Mass.: Harvard University Press, 1994), 73.

42. Jin, "Xinsh ji Zhongguo Zhengzhi Gaige Ruogan Zhongda Wenti de Sikao," 30.

43. He Ping and Liu Siyang, "Dang de Xinyijie Zhongyang Weiyuanhui Danshengji" [The Birth of the New Central Committee of the CCP], available at www.xinhuanet.com, accessed on November 14, 2002.

44. Lianjiang Li, "The Two-Ballot System in Shanxi Province: Subjecting Village Party Secretaries to a Public Vote," *The China Quarterly*, no. 42 (1999): 107.

45. Wang Bangzuo and Xie Yue, "Zhengdang Tuidong: Zhongguo Zhengzhi Tizhi Gaige de Yanzhang Luoji" [Party's Initiative: Logic of Chinese Political Reform], *Chinese Politics*, no. 8 (2001): 17; Jin, "Xinshi ji Zhongguo Zhengzhi Gaige Ruogan Zhongda Wenti de Sikao," 28; Xiong Gang, "Lun Woguo Zhengzhi Tizhi Gaige de Lishi Yanjin he Zouxiang" [On the Development and Future Trend of China's Political

Reform], *Zhongguo Zhengzhi*, no. 1 (2002): 18; Ye Weishi, "Sange Daibiao Zhongyao Sixiang Xingcheng he Fazhang Mailuo."

46. Jiang, "Report to the 16th National Party Congress."

47. Li Zhongjie, "Yi Gaige de Jingsheng Ba Dang de Jianshe Tuixiang Qianjin" [Promoting Party-Building with the Reform Spirit], available at www.xinhuanet.com, accessed on September 11, 2002.

48. Wang et al., *Xinshiji Dang de Jianshe de Weida Gangling*, 128.

49. Barrington Moore, *Social Origins of Dictatorship and Democracy* (Boston: Beacon Press, 1966); Robert Dahl, *Democracy and Its Critics* (New Haven, Conn.: Yale University Press, 1989), 251.

50. Yasheng Huang, "Why China Will Not Collapse," *Foreign Policy*, no. 99 (1995): 54–68.

51. Yan Renkuan, "Beijing Zhengtan Disandai" [Beijing's Third-Generation Politicians], *Tide Monthly* (Hong Kong), 52 (1991): 12.

52. Weng Jieming et al., eds., *Yu Zongshuji Tanxin* [Talking with the General Secretary] (Beijing: Zhongguo Shehui Kexue Chubanshe, 1996).

53. John Pomfret, "Chinese Capitalists Gain New Legitimacy: Ties to State Pay Off for Some Ventures," *Washington Post*, September 29, 2002, A01.

54. Deng Xiaoping, *Selected Works of Deng Xiaoping: 1975–1982* (Beijing: Renmin Chubanshe, 1983), 289.

55. "Deng's Ideas on Political Restructuring," *Beijing Review* 30, no. 39, September 28, 1987.

56. Zhu Guanglei, *Dangdai Zhongguo Zhengfu Guocheng* [Process of Government in Contemporary China] (Tianjin: Tianjin Renmin Chubanshe, 1997), 77.

57. Richard Baum, "To Reform or to Muddle Through? The Challenges Facing China's Fourth Generation," in *Asia Program Special Report* 105: *The 16th CCP Congress and Leadership Transition in China*, ed. Gang Lin and Susan Shirk (Washington, D.C.: Woodrow Wilson International Center for Scholars, 2002), 39.

58. M. Kent Jennings, "Political Participation in the Chinese Countryside," *American Political Science Review* 91, no. 2 (1997): 361.

Chapter 3

The State and the Private Sector in a New Property Rights System

Xiaobo Hu

Property rights as an institution provide incentives, shape behaviors, and protect interests. The emerging property rights system in China has provided a new foundation for state–private sector interactions in the post-Jiang era. After decades of gradual yet sweeping transformation of China's property rights system, the fourth generation of Chinese leadership faces a fundamentally new relationship with the economy, with the society, and perhaps more importantly, with growing pressure groups in China. The "Three Represents" reflects an initial state strategy at the beginning of this new relationship. This process is by no means smooth, but rather filled with contradictions.

In this chapter, I explore how this new relationship between the state and private sector has evolved through a property rights perspective. I examine the institutional roots of this new relationship, and argue that such relationship will continue for the foreseeable future. The importance of path dependency in institution building is emphasized. Along with institution building or innovation, the notion of path dependency points to the constraints as well as the opportunities that have been framed by preexisting rules and norms for political actors. The new institutions created will frame new constraints and new opportunities for future political interactions. Through a series of institutional innovations, recent Chinese political and economic reforms have provided better or more benefits for some groups than for others. Political reshufflings excluded groups of people from the next round of redistribution of benefits. The new middle class, dominated by a combination of former bureaucrats of all ranks, emerged as the utmost beneficiaries of this property rights transformation.

This chapter surveys the process of property rights transformation in China in the past two decades, and then investigates the beneficiaries of this historical transformation. In the third section, I discuss the emerging system and the major issues generated through this transformation. Two new issues—land reform and employment—must be tackled promptly and carefully in post-Jiang China.

The State of Changing Property Rights

Although property rights are often regarded as exclusive ownership over property, the subject matter of property rights can usefully be analyzed as comprised of three components, including user rights, extractor rights, and seller rights.[1] User rights allow agents to use the assets without necessarily claiming ownership, extractor rights are rights to returns from the assets, and seller rights are rights to transfer the assets. There are a variety of ways in which such a disaggregation of property rights might be enforced.[2] Extractor rights are similar to the "residual control rights" defined by Sanford J. Grossman and Oliver D. Hart,[3] but they specifically refer to individuals' rights to extract personal rewards.

In reality, the three components of property rights are not always in the hands of the same agents all the time. In fact, separation of the three components can be seen as a major characteristic of economic reforms in China and Central and Eastern Europe.[4] Since the late 1970s in China, each economic reform has transformed parts of property rights. To be precise, this process has gradually transformed parts of each component of property rights over state assets from the hands of the central government to local governments, to state-owned enterprises, and then to individuals. The transformation started with user rights, and then "spilled over" to extractor rights, and will finally be concluded in the realization of seller rights. It has been a piecemeal transformation.

Solutions to the Problem of Low Productivity

In the late 1970s, the Chinese central government adopted a new agricultural production model initiated by a poor village in Anhui Province and introduced this model to the peasantry as the Household Responsibility System. The system was intended to solve the problems of low productivity in rural China by providing peasants with "materialistic" incentives. In two ways the new rural incentive system started a gradual transformation of user rights. First, the system gave permission for peasants to work independently—not as a team or collective—in order to fulfill state targets. It later encouraged peasants to make their own production decisions on how to fulfill state targets. For example, peasants were allowed to decide what kind of seeds they would purchase and how much and what kind of fertilizer they would apply. This therefore expanded peasant user rights over the land, which I will discuss further below. Second, this system was initially implemented in limited areas, and then gradually spread to almost all corners of the Chinese countryside. According to China's State Statistics Bureau, the percentage of rural households that adopted the Responsibility System increased from 1 percent in 1979 to 14 percent in 1980, 45 percent in 1981, 80 percent in 1982, 98 percent in 1983, and 99 percent in 1984.[5]

When the Household Responsibility System was shown to be successful, the Chinese central government launched the Contract Responsibility System in 1982 in an attempt to further improve agricultural production. While the Chinese leaders intended to revitalize the economy within the state planning system, the new system in effect expanded further peasant user rights over the land. Under this system, peasants have gained additional freedom to choose what to grow and when to grow on the land assigned to them.

The economic reform that started in the mid-1980s in urban China paralleled what had happened in rural China in terms of expansion of user rights over state assets. It is usually referred to as part of the decentralization reform, in which the central government delegated decision-making authority first to local governments and then to state-owned enterprises.

In 1984, the central government started to expand the scope of its reform experiment for reform with the Factory Manager Responsibility System in urban China. At the beginning of implementing the new system, the managers were given responsibility over choices of managerial models or incentive systems. Responsibility was then extended to choices over suppliers for the purchase of raw materials, to choices over the markets for selling products, and finally to choices of products to be produced.[6] The percentage of state-owned enterprises that adopted the management responsibility system also grew step by step, from 2 percent in 1984, 4 percent in 1985, 8 percent in 1986, 42 percent in 1987, and 83 percent in 1988, to 88 percent in 1989.[7] Under this system, user rights over state assets were gradually delegated to more and more managers, who then could use state capital, infrastructure, and other resources to fulfill state production targets.

In 1986, the central government introduced the Long-Term Contracting System in order to increase the time horizon of managers' responsibilities—user rights—over state assets. In 1988, the Enterprise Law was adopted and it has since provided legal protection for user rights that all managers of state-owned enterprises could enjoy. The "Fourteen Articles" (see Appendix) issued by the central government in 1992 seemed to transfer all user rights over state-owned enterprises to the managers. Indeed, in an attempt to solve the economic problem of low productivity within the socialist system, the state started to transfer user rights to certain groups of individuals. The new user rights provided incentives to, and protected the interests of, these individuals.

Increasing Output

Another way the Chinese government increased the overall output of the economy was to establish a dual-track price system. Implemented from the mid-1980s to the early 1990s, this system was supposed to create an incentive mechanism to increase production. That is, the enterprise, after fulfilling the state quota, could produce and sell extra products to the market at a higher price. The state provided necessary resources at a low internal or planned price for the enterprise to meet the state target. According to Neil Gregory, Stoyan Tenev, and Dileep Wagle, this dual-track approach might have been "the most important aspect of Chinese reform since it was, at the time, an innovative solution to the political constraints on the direction and speed of reform."[8]

The dual-track system, however, prescribed two markets in the Chinese economy: one for the state sector and the other the non-state sector; one for the planned economy and the other for the rest. The operation of these two markets created a price gap that offered opportunities for bureaucrats and managers of state-owned enterprises to extract additional income from business dealings. For instance, managers could obtain supplies from the state at a lower, planned price and sell them to the market at the clearing price. Since the transaction was outside the state plan, the gain would not be returned to the state bureau—nor would it be entered into the enterprise's record of profits. With this dual-track approach, both bureaucrats in charge of resource allocation and managers of state-owned enterprises usually managed to save some amount of the planned resources and then sold them at a higher price to the market. Profits or surplus generated through such transactions were for bureaucrats and managers to keep. In this sense, the dual-track system provided opportunities for informal extraction from state assets. In other words, the state created informal extractor rights for bureaucrats and managers.

New studies stress that the behavior of socialist bureaucrats is decisively influenced by the rents that they receive from their interference in, or predation upon, profit-generating businesses.[9] Rent seeking exists in China in a different form since the "rent" is contrived through government planning. This contrived rent seeking extended the informal exercise of extractor rights to bureaucrats and managers for private returns. Recent studies by Angang Hu and others indicate that bureaucrats and managers have accumulated large profits within a short period of time.[10] I return to this matter in the next section.

Extractor rights are a major component of the property rights, similar to the "residual control rights" discussed by Grossman and Hart.[11] In the Chinese transformation, the privatization of extractor rights started with informal practices in government economic reform programs. This form of extractor rights brought about business deals under the table.

Promotion of Tertiary Sector

In the 1980s, privatization was a taboo in China, and extractor rights were not legally protected except for those in the hands of the state. In effect, the exercise of informal extractor rights meant law breaking or corruption. It thrived in a rather gray area of the Chinese economy.[12] The systems that induced such operations were all legal, but the operations themselves were not formally protected. This was one of the paradoxes of the economic reforms.

On the other hand, the government decision to speed up development of the tertiary sector in effect extended informal extractor rights to many more people. For the government, development of the tertiary sector would resolve such problems as surplus labor force, capital shortage, lack of services, and low productivity. From a political perspective, by such a development policy, the government could gain support and loyalty because the tertiary sector transferred extractor rights to powerful individuals and created informal extractor rights for those who had influence over policymaking or policy implementation. For instance, in the late 1980s, every single Chinese work unit could typically use state properties—land, capital, and infrastructure—to set up trading companies and other companies in the service sector. These companies would not be supported by state finances, and hence would not be included in the state plan or put under the state control. Managers of the new businesses could act as de facto owners and extract additional income in the form of bonuses, commissions, or dividends.

One major area for rapid growth of informal extractor rights was in township and village collective enterprises. Township governments and village communities became involved in collective enterprises in their communities and were regarded as de facto owners. They provided start-up capital and hired managers. The enterprise's activities were not included in the state plan or put under the state control. Therefore, the reward system was determined by the community officials and managers themselves with a very flexible accounting system. Few restrictions were placed or guidance given on how the budget could be spent. In effect, officials and managers had the de facto rights to extract income from these collective enterprises, just like managers and urban bureaucrats had from their companies in the tertiary sector.

The directive issued by the Chinese Communist Party (CCP) Central Committee and the State Council in the early summer of 1992 and the 14th Party Congress convened later that year further extended the benefits of informal extractor rights to middle-ranking officials. Tax reform adopted in 1994 could be in this sense a legal outlet for money laundering that involved gains through exercise of informal extractor rights. A typical practice has been to keep gray earnings by paying taxes on them through a nonstate business account.

The development of the tertiary sector and rural collective enterprises in the late 1980s and early 1990s thus transferred extractor rights to individuals—bureaucrats and managers—without formal recognition. Again, in an attempt to solve economic problems while trying to hold on to political power, the state informally transferred extractor rights to certain groups of individuals, hence creating a new middle class in China. I return to this last issue later in this chapter.

Casting Off Financial Burdens

When you cannot fix it, desert it—that sounds like the working philosophy for the Chinese government. When it could not solve the problems of inefficiency in state-owned enterprises, the state first transferred the resultant budget deficit to state banks by requiring the latter to continue the bad loans (*daizhang, huaizhang, sizhang*). When the government banks could not continue without going bankrupt, the state started to look for other "victims" through shareholding, merger, and sales. This is the process of economic problem solving in China in the eyes of some Chinese economists. However, through shareholding, merger, bankruptcy, and sales, the state has been transferring the last major component of property rights—seller rights—to individuals, employees, and managers.

Transformation of seller rights did not really start until 1997 when the government launched a new round of economic reforms to renovate and retain large state-owned enterprises and to privatize smaller ones (*zhuada fangxiao*). Before 1997, the shareholding system launched in 1984 and the Bankruptcy Law adopted in 1986 had started to define the state's responsibility and to limit the state's liability in state-owned enterprises, while the Enterprise Law effective in 1988 started to clarify a distinct legal status for state-owned enterprises.

However, the Fifth Session of the 8th National People's Congress and the 15th Party Congress, both convened in 1997, initiated a new round of economic reforms aimed at improving the state sector and "letting go" of state-owned enterprises that could not be revitalized—especially medium- to small-sized enterprises. A wave of mergers swept across the country in 1997, with mergers of some 3,000 large enterprises and reorganization of some 15.5 billion yuan in state assets. In 1997, in order to smooth the process, the State Council provided a one-time fund of 30 billion yuan to clear some of the debt of bankrupt enterprises.

The relative smooth process of the new round of economic reform might have "quietly" revolutionized the property rights system in China by completing the piecemeal transformation, and by uniting all three components of property rights, this time into the hands of property owners. Before 1997, the right to sell production assets was controversial and seriously restricted by the state. Even transfers between government agencies were not taken in the form of exchange of values, not to mention an open auction in a market competition. The pre-1997 "rights to transfer assets" in the two areas discussed by Andrew Walder cannot be considered as seller rights.[13] They were extractor rights realized in sales of products or user rights to subcontracting. The seller rights refer to *the owner's right* to total alienation from the asset with or without compensation.[14]

Policy changes in 1997, however, have started to establish such owner's rights through formal merger, shareholding, and sales. The Provisional Measure for the Merger of Enterprises promulgated in 1989 states, "The merger of enterprises refers to an action in which an enterprise purchases the property rights of another enterprise, making it lose or change its status as a legal entity."[15] The new round of economic activities aimed at ridding the state of financial burdens began to transfer "owner's rights" to private citizens.

Indeed, the new rights of the user, extractor, and seller are by-products of decades-long Chinese economic reforms. When they started the epic economic reform, the Chinese communist leaders never had in mind any plan to transfer "owner's rights" to private citizens. However, through a series of reforms aiming at solving the economic problems of the time, China has transferred the three components of property rights piece by piece and step by step to non-state actors. More importantly, in retrospect, these by-products have been the major locomotives for the transformation of the property rights system in China. More medium- to small-sized state-owned enterprises were privatized than larger ones. Hence, when it privatized the medium- to small-sized state-owned enterprises, the state created an emerging business class, with more private owners than managers of state-owned enterprises. While the transformation is close to completion, the state needs to tackle new issues and new problems.

Insider Benefits

In *Privatizing Russia*, Maxim Boycko, Andrei Shleifer, and Robert Vishny assert that "the claim of employees on the shares of their firms was recognized in Russia from the start."[16] It is plausible that in a relatively more democratic and open system like Russia (vis-à-vis China), millions of employee-voters comprised a strong interest group in privatization policymaking. However, the power of managers must not be ignored. Russian managers "controlled a powerful lobby in the Parliament, Arkady Volsky's Civic Union." Indeed, the authors of *Privatizing Russia* also realize that "despite the fact that managers stood to gain a lot from privatization, they were in a position to bargain for even more."[17]

Despite differences in the pace of economic reforms—that is, radicalism versus gradualism—the privatization process and those who have benefited the most in the process have been very similar across China and other former socialist countries. The pattern of who enjoys more property rights or other benefits resulting from economic reform reveals a high degree of path dependency. In other words, de facto right holders have enjoyed more benefits—it is a business of insiders, or a political economy of insiders.

Not everyone involved in the process in China qualifies as "insiders." For instance, Chinese peasants enjoyed only momentarily the benefits created through the new user rights that were transferred to them by the state in the late 1970s and early 1980s. The peasants were first allowed to adopt the Household Responsibility System and other contracting systems. When it created and transferred new user rights to the peasants, the state received political support from them. However, the rural transformation stagnated at this first stage; therefore, the peasants lost their comparative advantage soon after the early 1980s.

On the other hand, the creation and transformation of user rights in urban areas have generated lasting benefits for de facto right-holders. Implementing state policies and production plans, government bureaucrats and managers of state-owned enterprises were the de facto right holders at the time when China started to reform. The reform in the 1980s started to "train" these people to make rational and accountable decisions, compete in a quasi-market environment, and accumulate experience that would be useful later when they were turned into private owners.

Through the expansion of informal extractor rights, government bureaucrats, state business managers, and directors of township and village collective enterprises were all provided opportunities to accumulate their own wealth. Quite a few government bureaucrats enjoyed more benefits by either sitting on the board of directors, engaging in jobs other than their own, or establishing new businesses out of state assets. Quite a few state business managers did the same in addition to keeping some profits in a separate account—"the small gold reservoir *(xiao jin ku)*"—for themselves. In addition, quite a few rural officials and directors had much more flexibility and treated collective enterprises like their own family businesses. When the state launched reform programs such as the dual-track system and the development of the tertiary sector, they were ardent supporters. In other cases, when the government needed political support—for example, early 1992 during and immediately after Deng Xiaoping's visit to South China—it could introduce such reform programs and new property rights in order to generate support from a targeted population. These reform policies created a class of "bureau-preneurs," who were holding dual positions as both government bureaucrats and business managers in the non-state sector. Their interests in bureaucracy and business were enhanced by informal extractor rights.

This class has grown quickly through the transformation of seller rights since the mid-1990s. It has become a class of bureaucrats transformed into entrepreneurs. The *zhuada fangxiao* policy of the late 1990s mentioned early in this chapter has provided a window to examine this evolution.

In most of the cases of transformation, medium- to small-sized state-owned enterprises and township and village collective enterprises have been sold to their previous directors and managers. An example is an industrial district in Shenyang, Liaoning Province, northern China. The municipal district of Huanggu had sold forty-one state-owned or collective enterprises within its jurisdiction by summer 2000. Seventy-one percent were sold to their own directors, formerly the de facto right holders. An example of a rural town is Changjing in Jiangsu Province, southern China. Changjing had transformed 191 collective enterprises by summer 2002. Except for eight enterprises that have been discontinued, almost all the rest of these enterprises are now in the hands of their former directors or managers, in one form or another. The transformation of these enterprises has taken a variety of forms, including shareholding, leasing, layaway, and internal transfers.[18]

These two examples reveal the beneficiaries of the latest transformation. Yet, as suggested in the previous discussion, tracing the path dependency back to the beginning of the reforms and revealing how insiders continue to do well in the Chinese transformation of property rights are straightforward.

Property rights transformation in China originated in previous institutions where the holders of political authority controlled virtually all aspects of society. Previous reforms prepared the ground for the rise of a bureaucrat-manager class, which in turn set up a clear path for privatization in which these bureaucrats and managers could efficiently continue to make profits out of the transition itself. In the initial phase of the transformation, socialist egalitarianism favored those who were holding the power and position—those bureaucrats and managers—to benefit from their new rights. Through path dependency, early reform policies and practice opened up new avenues for certain groups of people but closed the door to many others. Interestingly, retired revolutionary veterans couldn't enjoy user rights and extractor rights, although their children might, because the rights were transferred to the de facto right holders. To be precise, during the transformation, the de facto right holders were in the best position to obtain, exercise, and keep the newly created rights to themselves. Workers were not among this privileged group, nor were

peasants. In the late 1980s and the first half of the 1990s, those who controlled the allocation of state assets were the ones who could enjoy informal rights: They are de facto user right holders. Those "who were in the
right place at the right time" could enjoy them: They emerged soon after
the Cultural Revolution as a new generation of political elites. They were
chief officers in government bureaus and state-owned enterprises, and
they supported reforms.

These chief officers extended their managerial authority during the decentralization reforms in the 1980s. They turned out to be the major beneficiaries under the contracting and responsibility systems. They profited
through dual-track prices. They gained their ultimate economic freedom
while developing the newly emergent tertiary sector and township and village collective enterprises. In these sectors, they were either "investors" by
reallocating the retained profits and state assets to new enterprises, or they
were de facto owners—legal representatives of the state or state-owned enterprises (*faren daibiao*)—running the new enterprises. In a recent study of
Chinese collective enterprises, Guoqiang Tian affirms that the administrative bureaucrats hold special resources that give them a comparative advantage in transitional economies.[19] Contracting, responsibility, and dual-
track systems then gave them chances to experience risk taking, explore
market mechanisms, and accumulate private capital. When the time came,
they were the chosen ones as up-front beneficiaries in forming private
properties out of state assets.

While the market was not entirely open or economic activities were
largely regulated by bureaucrats, the exercise of informal extractor rights
made economic transactions more efficient. In such cases, those who could
enjoy user rights (i.e., enterprise managers), and those who represented the
owner (i.e., government bureaucrats), could collude and exercise the de
facto yet informal extractor rights for bureaucrats by including the latter in
the distribution of the enterprise's profits. For instance, influential government officials would be enlisted in the company's board of directors and
receive regular commissions in return. The beneficiaries of such a system
are its natural advocates. In many other cases where rules limit the users'
income level, the users themselves are the main driving forces to push for
informal extractor rights. As long as policymakers and those officials who
implement policies can benefit from it, they become acquiescent to the exercise of informal extract rights.

In the final process of transferring seller rights, bureaucrats and
mangers proceed to redistribute the "social valuables" in their favor and

exclude other people from sharing them. What we have seen in the cases of
Shenyang and Changjing is not unique, but a typical practice in the distribution of insider benefits. Typically, the supervising agency of the state or
collective enterprise would actively engage in identifying "proper" potential buyers of the enterprise. Not surprisingly, it has admitted that incumbent directors or managers were its first preference. In this sense, property
rights transformation has also been a process of transferring state rights
and assets to a certain group of people, former bureaucrats and state managers. In this process, it produced a business and managerial class out of
former government bureaucrats and managers of state-owned and collective enterprises.

The Mixed System: A New Class and Two New Issues

As a result of more than two decades of transformation, a new system has
emerged with a mixed arrangement of economic relationships, that is, a
mixed economy at the macro level. The state is controlling, and will try to
maintain control over, the largest enterprises and to continue to dominate
the major economic sectors. Private business will flourish, especially in
the gray areas between the state sector and the market and in the areas the
state is interested in providing protection against foreign takeovers. As the
gray areas become transparent, property rights will be more clearly defined
and protected by all players, including the state. China's accession to
WTO ever widens the Chinese door to the outside world and will bring
home major multinational corporations as well as fierce competition.[20] The
foreign "devils" have already arrived. For example, investment in China
by U.S. firms has increased from $200 million in 1989 to $7.8 billion in
2000.[21] There are currently more than 33,000 U.S. companies in China.[22]

While selling medium- to small-sized state-owned enterprises to private
owners and encouraging foreign companies to invest in China, the state
has managed to keep many large enterprises. It has pursued this as a state
policy or as the economic reform of *zhuada fangxiao*—that is, to renovate
and retain large state-owned enterprises and to privatize smaller ones. The
state may have to keep these large enterprises even though some of them
have continued to run up deficits and some others need to be shut down.
But the state has its dilemmas. First of all, the Party, which controls the
state, wants to stay in office. If the country were dominated by private
business, then the Party would lose its legitimacy to rule. Second, if it
could not control these large enterprises, the state would have difficulties
dominating selected industries or implementing Party policies. After ac-

cession to WTO, it seems more important for the state to maintain control over major economic sectors in order for it to implement its protective policies. Finally, these large enterprises have retained many workers who are potential sources of major social unrest if the enterprises go bankrupt or if the workers are laid off. If such dilemmas remain, the state sector will continue to have a place in the new economic system.

Although the private sector has increased dramatically in recent years (see Figure 3.1), it will not replace the state and collective sectors in the foreseeable future. Jiang Zemin urged the leadership to "consolidate and develop unswervingly the public [i.e., state] sector of the economy" in his political report to the 16th Party Congress.[23] The original collective sector may turn into shareholding or public enterprises, but it may not step down from the historical stage very soon, simply because quite a few local governments depend on it for generating revenue. However, scholars still argue that the division of state versus non-state ownership has yet been clearly defined. *The Economist* maintains that China's property rights "are so hazy that it is still unclear whether Legend—[China's biggest computer maker]—is a state-owned, collective, or private enterprise."[24]

This exemplifies a mixed arrangement of economic relationships within many companies, that is, a mixed economy at the micro level. At the end of property rights transformation, many large shareholding companies are

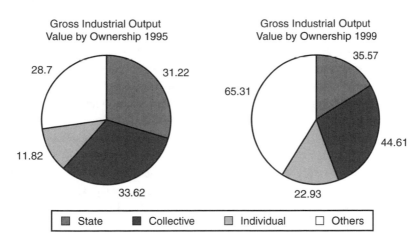

Figure 3.1. *Changes in national percentages of ownership types, 1995 to 1999.*
Source: China Internet Information Center, available at www.china.org.cn/ e-Internet/JJ/HTM/13-1.htm, accessed on September 17, 2002.

dominated by the state's shares—the state controls more than 50 percent of the shares. Other shares are typically divided among the company's managers and employees, and other state-owned enterprises. Participation in shareholding by private companies has increased recently and seems to continue growing. This is a new system of mixed shareholding at the microeconomic level.

In such a mixed economy, each player will look for its position and edge to thrive. Conflicts will arise between state-owned enterprises and private businesses over resources and preferential treatment. The state needs to handle this competition carefully, balancing incentives for both parties. To the state, both sectors are very important. The state sector provides a necessary policy tool and indispensable outlet for surplus workers. The private sector provides much economic growth as well as job opportunities.

On the other hand, the two sectors may join in a coalition and push the government for further economic reforms, especially reforms that favor business owners and managers, such as lower taxes and soft loans; or those minimizing the power of the employees, such as blocking collective bargaining. A coalition may also arise between the two sectors in the gray areas, where both can collude and benefit at the expense of the state and the market. The "hazy" property rights then seem doomed to last. There is no clear answer to the question of whether the Chinese stockholders will really enjoy the same full rights as those in a mature market economy.

In the face of foreign competition, the state and private sectors may join each other against multinational corporations. Many private owners are former government bureaucrats or state business managers. They have a long-term close relationship with the state sector. Their network may engage them in reciprocal support. The state is also interested in supporting domestic industries, in which private investment has become a vital part. A triangular coalition among the state, state-owned enterprises, and private business might yield a protectionist model similar to Japan's.[25]

However, the state sector and the private sector may also compete to take advantage of multinational corporations, especially when the latter could bring in international capital and new technology. If so, the state may be at the risk of losing a desirable balance, because such large multinational corporations, with help from local interests, could easily cripple the economic policies of a developing country like China.

A new triangular relationship may also be established among state-owned enterprises, private businesses, and the multinationals. The multinationals may easily manipulate the triangle with the magnitude of their business operations. Currently, many examples only involve money laundering for the state managers, hence resulting in a serious loss of state assets and state wealth.[26] At this stage, due to the lack of collective bargaining power of the private sector in China's central decision-making process, state-owned enterprises and multinationals would get an upper hand. Private domestic businesses may be considered as a lesser partner at this moment.

However, the state has to face a new class, dominated by private owners or quasi-private owners—that is, state-owned enterprise managers who have engaged in non-state sectors and share similar interests with private owners. They are also former friends or colleagues of government bureaucrats. These people will seek out all possible ways to exert influence over the state.

Indeed, the emerging middle class in China, different from that in many other third world countries, is not dominated by highly paid technical staff employed by the multinationals, but by three groups: state-owned enterprise managers, local private owners, and multinational employees. The last group is currently small but growing fast after China's accession to WTO. In addition, the academic elite, such as professors and researchers from top universities and research institutions, can also be considered visible members of the middle class. One may be able to argue that the current Chinese capitalist accumulation is different from the Western one. The Chinese capitalists have accumulated their initial capital through domestic resource reallocation rather than through imperialism. If so, then one should be able to argue that the composition of the Chinese new middle class is vastly different from that in the West as well.

As discussed above, the emergence of China's middle class has resulted from a series of economic reforms. Will this path of dependency be stopped in post-Jiang China? It is highly unlikely. The CCP has already decided to recruit new members from this pool of the population. The private owners are now recorded as making significant contributions to advancing productivity, productive relationships, and overall economic development. According to one report, 100,000 businesspeople have joined the Party since the ban on private owners—capitalists—was lifted in 2001.[27] In addition, a few private owners were brought into the 16th Party Congress as delegates who "elected" the most powerful Chinese in China for the next generation.[28]

The new mixed economic system has produced a new middle class in

China. Together with the new middle class, it has also produced many new issues and challenging problems. Let us turn to focus on two of them here. These two are urgent and closely related to the emergence of the mixed economic system.

First, the rural transformation of property rights has stagnated at the first stage whereby user rights are still very limited and land sales are not permitted. However, discussions and debates concerning seller rights over land have already started by researchers in universities and research institutions across China. In the transformation of property rights where urban enterprises realize the importance of the land, the bureaucrats and managers started to push for seller rights to the land. The state may have also realized that the next step to release the productive energy of rural China might be to grant seller rights over land use, although not of the land itself. Recently, China adopted the Rural Land Contracting Law, which represented a breakthrough for the land-tenure rights of China's 210 million farm families. The new law was to strengthen the land use rights for farmers for thirty years within one generation and to provide the foundation for markets in rural land use rights. While key issues remain to be addressed, hopefully through additional legislation, the new law "provides an extraordinary foundation for increased investment, productivity, and efficiency by Chinese farmers."[29] While state-owned enterprises have already divided up urban land among themselves, new private businesses have yet to advance their crusade into the countryside, where farmers are far from their competitors. With the addition of business leaders to the CCP Central Committee, the interests of private owners will be clearly represented.

A second issue, less fundamental than the first one but more urgent, is that the mixed economic system has already produced more than 6 million laid-off workers. It is expected that, in the first five years after China becomes a member of the WTO, there will be another 5 million workers being laid off. As a control mechanism over the macroeconomy, the state currently still maintains considerable power over the hiring and firing decisions of newly privatized enterprises. This is another paradox for China. On one hand, without such a post-transformation state intervention, the new enterprises will logically improve their productivity by firing surplus labor. This would increase the chance of social unrest, given that the state has limited funds to handle such a large troop of the unemployed, which would in turn worsen the environment for investment and economic development. Such problems have led the municipal governments in quite a few cities to reverse the privatization process—that is, municipal governments bought back the former state-owned enterprises it recently sold to the private owners. On the other hand, such post-transformation state interventions would render the transformation incomplete. Private owners and investors naturally wonder how far the state would go in order to maintain a "healthy environment for investment" at the expense of a sound property rights system.

These two problems are by no means easy to handle or quickly solved. They will occupy the attention and energy of the new generation of Chinese leadership at least for their initial years.

Conclusion

Five years ago after the 15th Party Congress, scholars started to predict that the 16th Party Congress would be more open-minded regarding economic transformation and might openly push wholesale privatization.[30] Indeed, China had pursued wholesale privatization, especially in rural and in medium- to small-sized urban enterprises, in that five-year period. But the state leadership did this because it believed that such transformation would save the Party from losing power. The private sector will be allowed to "play an important role in mobilizing the initiative of all quarters of the society to quicken the development of the productive forces,"[31] which is much needed by the Party in order to stay in power.

The new state leadership, no matter who controls the agenda, may not move fast enough in political reforms, because it has to consolidate its power base first,[32] especially when Party General Secretary Hu Jintao may have to face a large block of potential challengers. In its early years, the new leadership will sort out friends and foes, and then decide on a new incentive system for the population. However, the two abovementioned urgent issues that the state has to deal with immediately will generate instant policy debates. Along with the prospect of possible intra-party democratization discussed in Chapter 2, the state has to balance between social order and economic growth. Naturally, the new middle class would try to preserve the latter. On the other hand, "establishment theoretician Kang Xiaoguang, a well-known professor at Tsinghua University, admitted that the Party had no choice but to bolster its links with the [business] elite."[33]

Well-known political dissident Bao Tong, former advisor to the ousted premier Zhao Ziyang, has questioned whether the "Three Represents" will represent what the phrase indicates. Or, will the "Three Represents" really represent only the rich, the powerful, and the fortunate—those bureaucrats and managers "in the right place at the right time?" This is an important question that no one can afford to ignore. From the perspective of path dependency, the answer depends on the current institutional arrangement of power, and the answer will also set the stage for a new round of benefits sharing. But it is certain, as Jiang Zemin put it, that "the non-public sector of self-employed, private and other forms of ownership is an important component part of the socialist market economy."[34]

Notes

This research was supported in part by a research grant from the Arthur M. Spiro Center for Entrepreneurial Leadership at Clemson University. I am grateful to Nicole Cariri for her invaluable research assistance, and to Gang Lin and Lowell Dittmer for their insightful comments on an early draft.

1. See Xiaobo Hu, *Problems in China's Transitional Economy: Property Rights and Transitional Models* (Singapore: Singapore University Press, 1998), and "Transformation of Property Rights in China: The Institutional Origins," Entrepreneurial Leadership Working Paper Series 02-101 (The Arthur M. Spiro Center for Entrepreneurial Leadership, Clemson University, Clemson, S.C., 2002); and Jean C. Oi and Andrew G. Walder, eds., *Property Rights and Economic Reform in China* (Stanford, Calif.: Stanford University Press, 1999).

2. Harold Demsetz, "Toward a Theory of Property Rights," in *Ownership, Control, and the Firm: The Organization of Economic Activity*, ed. Harold Demsetz (Oxford: Blackwell, 1967), 1:104–116.

3. Sanford J. Grossman and Oliver D. Hart, "The Costs and Benefits of Ownership: A Theory of Vertical and Lateral Integration," *Journal of Political Economy* 94 (1986): 691–719.

4. See William Byrd, *The Market Mechanism and Economic Reform in China* (Armonk, NY: M.E. Sharpe, 1991); Andrew G. Walder, "Corporate Organization and Local Government Property Rights in China," in *Changing Political Economies: Privatization in Post-Communist and Reforming Communist States*, ed. Vedat Milor (Boulder, Colo.: Lynne Rienner Publishers, 1994), 58–66; and Milica Uvalic and Daniel Vaughan-Whitehead, *Privatization Surprises in Transition Economies: Employee-Ownership in Central and Eastern Europe* (Cheltenham, UK: Edward Elgar Publishing Limited, 1997).

5. China's State Statistics Bureau, *Statistical Yearbook of China* (Beijing: China Statistical Publishing House, various years).

6. For detailed discussion, see Peter N.S. Lee, *Industrial Management and Economic Reform in China, 1949–1984* (Hong Kong: Oxford University Press, 1987); William Byrd, *Chinese Industrial Firms under Reform* (Washington, D.C.: World Bank, 1992); and Susan L. Shirk, *The Political Logic of Economic Reform in China* (Berkeley: University of California Press, 1993).

7. *Statistical Yearbook of China*, various years.

8. Neil Gregory, Stoyan Tenev, and Dileep Wagle, *China's Emerging Private Enterprises: Prospects for the New Century* (Washington, D.C.: International Finance Corporation, 2000), 7.

9. Jan Winiecki, "Why Economic Reforms Fail in the Soviet System: A Property Rights-Based Approach," *Economic Inquiry* 28 (1990): 195–221; Lawrence Lau, Yingyi Qian, and Gerard Roland, "Reform without Losers: An Interpretation of China's Dual-Track Approach to Transition," Discussion Paper 1798 (London: Center for Economic Policy Research, 1997); and Andrew G. Walder, "The State as an Ensemble of Economic Actors: Some Inferences from China's Trajectory of Change," in *Transforming Post-Communist Political Economies*, ed. Joan Nelson, Charles Tilly, and LeeWalker (Washington, D.C.: National Academy Press, 1998), 432–452.

10. Angang Hu, *China: Fighting Against Corruption* [in Chinese] (Hangzhou: Zhejiang People's Publishing House, 2001); and "TIME Magazine: Majority of Chinese Start-Ups Gain Wealth Illegally" [in Chinese], September 17, 2002, available at www.zaobao.com/special/newspapers/2002/09/others170902d.html, accessed on September 17, 2002.

11. Sanford J. Grossman and Oliver D. Hart, "The Costs and Benefits of Ownership: A Theory of Vertical and Lateral Integration," *Journal of Political Economy* 94 (1986): 691–719.

12. David D. Li, "A Theory of Ambiguous Property Rights in Transition Economies: The Case of the Chinese Non-State Sector," *Journal of Comparative Economics* 23 (1996): 1–19.

13. Milor, *Changing Political Economies*, 9.

14. Thráinn Eggertsson, *Economic Behavior and Institutions* (Cambridge: Cambridge University Press, 1990).

15. Shibai Liu, "Merger as an Important Form in Transforming Property Rights of the Enterprises" [in Chinese], *People's Daily*, February 3, 1989, p. 5.

16. Maxim Boycko, Andrei Shleifer, and Robert Vishny, *Privatizing Russia* (Cambridge, Mass.: MIT Press, 1997), 76.

17. Ibid., 77.

18. For a detailed discussion, see Hu, "Transformation of Property Rights in China."

19. Guoqiang Tian, "Property Rights and the Nature of Chinese Collective Enterprises," *Journal of Comparative Economics* 28 (2000): 247–268.

20. Lawrence C. Reardon "The Death Knell of China's Command Economy: The WTO and China's State-Owned Enterprises," *China Enters the WTO: The Death Knell for State-Owned Enterprises,* ed. Gang Lin, *Asia Program Special Report* 103 (Washington, D.C.: Woodrow Wilson International Center for Scholars, 2002), 7–10.

21. Franklin Crawford, "Cornell ILR Researcher: Trade with China Hurts U.S. Labor Market," *Cornell Chronicle*, August 30, 2001, available at www.news.cornell.edu/Chronicle/01/8.30.01/China_trade.html, accessed on September 16, 2002. Data from China's State Statistical Bureau, quoted by the U.S. Department of Commerce, shows that the U.S. realized foreign direct investment in China was $4.38 billion in 2000.

22. "US Domain Has Huge Demand in Asia," *PR Newswire*, April 24, 2002, available at www.onlinenic.com/english/news/olnews_20020424.html, accessed on September 16, 2002.

23. "Full Text of Jiang Zemin's Report at the 16th Party Congress, IV," November 8, 2002, Xinhuanet, available at www.xinhuanet.com, accessed on December 2, 2002; and Zhou Ruipeng, Li Huiling, and Sun Chuanwei, "Ownership System of State Enterprises Clearly Defined" [in Chinese], *Lianhe Zaobao*, November 9, 2002, p. 6. In the

same speech, Jiang also stated, "Expansion of the state sector and its control of the life-line of the national economy [are] of crucial importance..."

24. "Face Value Legend in the Making," *The Economist*, September 15, 2001, p. 64.

25. Chalmers Johnson, *MITI and the Japanese Miracle: The Growth of Industrial Policy, 1925–1975* (Stanford, Calif.: Stanford University Press, 1982); and Ezra Vogel, *Japan as Number One* (Cambridge, Mass.: Harvard University Press, 1979).

26. "Flight of Four Thousand Corrupt Officials" [in Chinese], *Industrial and Commercial Times*, August 24, 2002; and "Flight of Mainland Capital over $50 Million in Three Years," *China Times*, September 11, 2002.

27. Damien McElroy, "Jiang Stamps Authority with Five More Years at Top," *The Scotsman*, August 26, 2002, available at http://search.scotsman.com/scripts/rwisapi.dll/@network.env, accessed on August 29, 2002.

28. "China's Politburo 'Proposes' Convening 16th Party Congress 8 November," *Financial Times* (UK), August 25, 2002, available at http://news.ft.com, accessed on August 26, 2002.

29. "China Adopts Rural Land Contracting Law: A Breakthrough for Farmers' Land-Tenure Rights," *Monthly News & Notes*, September (Seattle, Wash.: Rural Development Institute, 2002).

30. Hu, *Problems in China's Transitional Economy*, 35.

31. "Full Text of Jiang Zemin's Report at the 16th Party Congress, IV."

32. For a detailed discussion, see David Bachman, "Succession, Consolidation, and Transition in China's Future," *Journal of Northeast Asian Studies* 15 (1996): 89–106.

33. Willy Wo-Lap Lam, "China's 'Dangerous' Class Divide Set to Stay," Cable Network News, September 3, 2002, available at http://cnn.com, accessed on September 3, 2002.

34. "Full Text of Jiang Zemin's Report at the 16th Party Congress, IV."

Appendix

The "Fourteen Articles" Promulgated by the Chinese Central Government in 1992

According to a decision made by the central government, the state-owned enterprises shall hold the responsibilities to:

1. Make their own production and business decisions
2. Set their own prices
3. Market their own products
4. Purchase raw materials for themselves
5. Decide on the use of the retained earnings
6. Control personnel management
7. Form partnerships and mergers
8. Dispose of assets in accordance with production requirements

9. Set wages and bonuses
10. Determine internal organization
11. Import and export
12. Make investment decisions
13. Assign labor
14. Refuse arbitrary levies and charges

Chapter 4

One Country, Three Systems: State-Society Relations in Post-Jiang China

Richard Madsen

In the past decade, China's social development has been highly uneven and full of paradoxes. On the one hand, rapid economic growth has created a burgeoning urban middle class, whose members enjoy a comfortable prosperity (*xiao kang*) and greater levels of personal freedom than ever before in Chinese history.[1] Central to this freedom are the abilities to choose one's occupation, to move between jobs, and even to start up one's own business. Members of this new middle class can take for granted the basic necessities of life, such as adequate food, clothing, and housing, and they can busy themselves with working out a sense of individual identity by making personal choices among the wide variety of status symbols produced by a consumer society.[2] Often the goods with the highest status are precisely those that are part of a global system of brand names, most of which are of U.S. provenance, such as Starbucks coffee, Nike shoes, and McDonalds hamburgers. It is tempting to conclude that this new middle class—increasingly working in gleaming modernist office buildings, restlessly seeking new ways to make money and to acquire status by wearing the latest fashions and developing cosmopolitan tastes in food and drink—is embracing the "American way of life."

The temptation, however, should be resisted. Although many of the aspirations of China's new middle class are indeed reflective of U.S. free-market ideology, individualism, and consumerism, these aspirations in China are expressed in a very different context. In the United States, the "American way of life" permeates almost the entire society and is sustained by almost all social institutions. In China it can be realized only among a middle class of managers, professionals, and successful entrepreneurs that constitutes less than 10 percent of the population. By anyone's standards, this is a sizable group—perhaps 100 million people—but it floats in a sea of 1.3 billion people, many of whom are poor (if not in an absolute sense, at least in terms of their rising expectations about what constitutes a decent life) and insecure. Moreover, middle-class aspirations toward individual freedom and personal fulfillment are incongruent with many of the institutions that dominate Chinese life, including the autocratic Communist Party, a residential permit system that restricts geographical mobility, state-owned enterprises that still employ about 40 percent of the urban workforce, and extended families and corporate lineages that structure much of rural life.

Under these circumstances, increasing economic growth can lead not to broadly shared prosperity but to intensified social conflicts. And the modernization of some sectors of society (defined here in terms of increased opportunities toward private personal autonomy coupled with public regulation by universalistic rules) contrasts with new forms of traditionalism (defined here in terms of subordination of the individual to corporate groups governed through informal, particularistic relationships) in other sectors. The air-conditioned world of McDonalds and Starbucks coexists with the gritty environments of laid-off workers, migrant laborers, and underemployed farmers. The values of individual enterprise and fair play coexist with many kinds of corruption and political manipulation.

This chapter presents an overview of Chinese society in transition under the leadership of the "fourth generation." It is a picture of a weakly united whole bound together through codependent relationships in a fragile equilibrium. To make sense of the contrasts and paradoxes of contemporary Chinese society, I will argue that it is useful to think of Chinese society as consisting of several incompatible social systems, each with a distinctive internal stratification system, a distinctive pattern of life courses, and a distinctive set of cultural understandings about the proper relationship between self and society. Although by no means completely compatible, the different components of each system have a mutual synergy that contrasts with their more tension-filled relationships with the other systems. Perhaps like partners in a bad marriage, the systems are "codependent"[3] with one another. They gain enough superficial, short-term benefits from one another that they avoid confronting their fundamental long-term incompatibility.

We can call the systems "third-world China," "socialist China," and "newly industrializing China."[4] The systems are ideal types, and nowhere correspond perfectly to empirical reality. They predominate in different geographical regions. Third-world China most aptly describes the inland areas of central and western China—mostly rural, based on family-labor agriculture, and in some places riven by ethnic and religious conflict. Socialist China most aptly describes the industrial northeast, still dominated by the legacy of large state-owned enterprises. The coastal areas of China, with their dynamic, export-oriented economic growth, most clearly fit the description of a newly industrializing economy. However, the systems are not neatly distinguishable by geography. For example, even in the coastal areas of China, one can find some of the social patterns that characterize third-world China and socialist China.

Relationships between the systems are mediated by such actors as corrupt officials, migrant laborers, and diversifying families. The ability of some people to move between these systems, I will argue, has helped to diffuse social conflict, but the overall relationship between the systems is inherently unstable. I will first present an account of each of the three systems, and then discuss the terms of their uneasy relationships with one another. Finally, I will discuss the implications of the resultant uneasy balance between contradictory forces for social stability and the transformation of political institutions.

Third-World China

In third-world China, social status is heavily dependent on one's position within families and corporate lineages. Although the acquisition of political power is dependent on formal approval by Party and state bureaucracies, the actual practice of power is so dependent on informal, personal ties to kin and community that many leaders can be "local emperors" who are beyond effective control by the state. A successful life course in this kind of social system begins and ends with dependence on a male-dominated family. A comfortable and honorable old age in particular depends on being taken care by one's adult sons and their wives. The system is justified by cultural values stressing the centrality of family, the importance of maintaining an orderly hierarchy of family authority, and the mutual obligations of family members toward one another.

This system fits well the requirements of small-scale, labor-intensive farming. In China, about 70 percent of the population—about 800 million people—resides in villages and most of them make a living by farming. The typical farm consists of a single household that has responsibility for cultivating about one *mu* (1/15th of a hectare) of land. The household consumes about two-thirds of what it produces and sells the rest in a market that is highly regulated by the state. A household typically consists of a husband and wife, their children, and the parents of the husband. Often the family lives in proximity to other families who share a common ancestor through the male line. The bonds of kinship entail important moral claims that facilitate cooperation among the related families, while encouraging them to see their interests as separate from nonrelated families. Women in this system are to some degree perpetual outsiders. They marry into their husband's family and lineage and have as their primary responsibility the carrying on of that lineage by producing male children. It is male children, committed to staying in their natal villages, whom parents have to rely upon to provide care in their old age. Such arrangements are broadly similar to those found in most agrarian societies.

Although this system is not a straightforward continuation of "traditional" Chinese society—pre-modern society was far too diverse and changeable to constitute a fixed "tradition"—certain elements of the present-day rural system undoubtedly resonate with longstanding cultural practices. The system predominates today, however, not simply because of historical inertia but because of specific institutional arrangements imposed by governments of the People's Republic of China. The Maoist regime was ideologically opposed to the "feudal" practices of the traditional Chinese family, and it suppressed many traditional family rituals. However, many of the Maoist organizational arrangements actually helped to preserve some basic features of such family life. The people's commune system effectively confined farmers to agricultural work and made it almost impossible for them to move away from their natal communities. Social security was almost entirely dependent on the mutual support of family members. The most pitiable residents of any village were invariably those who had to depend on meager government handouts in their old age because they had no living family members nearby.[5] Even when the Maoist regime crushed the traditional local elites, they reinforced the system of cultural categories upon which traditional elite rule had been based. By giving deposed "gentry"—landlords and rich peasants—an official bad class label and by making that label inheritable through the male line, the Maoists affirmed the continuing importance of kinship and the existence of a fixed hierarchy of political status.[6]

Under Deng Xiaoping's reforms, the people's communes were dismantled in the early 1980s. Farmers now had much more flexibility about how they were to manage their agricultural production and many more opportunities to move around in search of non-agricultural work, and they were subjected to much less ideological pressure. But the new institutional arrangements have preserved the most important features of the family-based agrarian political economy. The current system replaces collective ownership with a "household responsibility system," under which each household is given long-term use of a small piece of land, but not allowed to sell the land or put it to nonfarming use. This system of small-scale farming reinforces the familistic social system described above. Meanwhile, in the absence of ideologically driven attempts to eliminate traditional family customs, such customs as elaborate marriage and funeral rituals have had a revival.

Moreover, the "household registration system" further reinforced the commitment of farmers to their villages and their patriarchal corporate families. Under this system, it is impossible for a farmer to become an urban resident. As we shall see, a great many farmers have in fact migrated to cities, but they live and work there as sojourners, as undocumented aliens, without any rights to state-subsidized health care, education for their children, or retirement pensions. If they are to get such social welfare benefits at all, they have to return to their villages.

With no change on the horizon in either the household responsibility system or the household registration system, farmers have to orient their lives, as they have done for centuries, around maintaining strong families embedded in kinship networks. Therefore, even as China rapidly modernizes, as the Chinese scholar Cao Jinqing argues in an important recent book, there remains an important degree of continuity with the rural social system that flourished in late imperial China.[7]

There has also been change. But the most recent changes have intensified some of the most problematic aspects of the late imperial system rather than transcending the system. In the late imperial system, one became wealthy not by becoming a more efficient farmer but by obtaining a

Confucian education and gaining political access to the state. Having achieved such access, one could gain considerable wealth by demanding favors from ordinary farmers in return for paternalistically protecting some of their interests. When the Confucian ethic was strong, there might be some genuine reciprocity between the local "gentry" and ordinary farmers, especially those connected through extended kinship with the local elite. By the end of the imperial era, however, the relationship had often become harshly exploitative and during the revolution, Communist organizers could mobilize farmers against "evil gentry."

During the 1990s, many of the old exploitative patterns began to return with a vengeance, result of the resurgence of aspects of traditional culture within a tightening rural economy. At the beginning of the household responsibility system in the early 1980s, there was a rapid growth of agricultural productivity. The quality of food and housing improved. The number of people living in what the United Nations would define as absolute poverty shrank to less than 10 percent of the population. But the rise in living standards raised expectations. And the spread of mass communications (about 80 percent of farm households now have televisions) made farmers ever more aware of widening gaps between countryside and city. Then, even as the overall Chinese economy began to grow at a spectacularly rapid rate in the mid-1990s, farmers' incomes began to plummet, a victim of declining prices for grain (kept low by the government's desire to stave off urban unrest) and rising prices for farm tools and fertilizer. Meanwhile, costs of medical care and education have risen beyond the capacity of many farmers to pay for them.

There is no way to improve the efficiency of farming without consolidating smallholdings into larger enterprises, an option precluded by the household responsibility system. Another hope for increasing farmers' incomes has been township and village enterprises (TVEs). These are local factories that can take advantage of cheap surplus labor. The TVEs are usually owned as joint stock companies by an entire community, but their profits often go mainly to the community's officials. In the late 1980s and early 1990s, they often produced enough income to offset diminishing returns to agriculture. But TVEs that are located far from city suburbs and lack adequate transportation infrastructure and managerial expertise have had a difficult time being profitable. In the late 1990s, most of them collapsed, leaving villages with debts and broken dreams.[8]

Under these circumstances, the most promising path to acquiring wealth for many farmers has seemed to be a traditional one—becoming an official and/or getting one's children an official post. The end of the old collective farming system was supposed to achieve some efficiency by shrinking the size of local government, and initially it did. But in the 1990s, the size of governments at the township and village level expanded over 400 percent. The income of these officials came from escalating fees imposed on local farmers in return for services of dubious value. In his *China Along the Yellow River*, Cao Jinqing cites some examples from extensive interviews he conducted in villages in Henan Province.[9] One town had 20 government and Party officials when it was organized as a people's commune in the 1970s. Now there are 150, about three-quarters of whom are probably superfluous. The local government sections that increased the most were those that brought in income from fines and taxes, such as family planning and public security.

In rural backwaters where "the heavens are high and the emperor far away," local officials, dependent more on local fees than a bureaucratic salary, not only ignore central government policies but sometimes turn them into their opposite. An example of such a perverse effect is the way the central government's family planning program has been implemented. To keep farmers from having more than one child (or two children if the first one was a girl), the family planning officials impose heavy fines, which many households are willing to pay because of the importance of having sons who will bear responsibility for taking care of the parents in old age. But since the local family planning officials depend on the fines (and probably bribes) for their income, they actually encourage the local farmers to have more children than the law allows.[10]

Within the past few years, the combination of a tightening rural economy and parasitical, exploitative officials has begun to reach a crisis point. In an angry letter published in the journal *Nanfang Zhoumo* (Southern Weekend) in August 2000, an honest local official complains that for some farmers net income has actually declined to below zero, because they cannot raise enough cash to pay their taxes and fees. The consequence has been widespread protests and sometimes rioting.[11] According to an article in the *South China Morning Post*, there were more than 2,000 "riots and other violent demonstrations against rural authorities" in 1999 alone.[12] And if anything, the numbers seem to have been increasing since then. Finally, in January 2002, an editorial in the *People's Daily* acknowledged that rural discontent was a serious threat to national stability and called for the government "to give more and take less from farmers, provide more service and less interference, and avoid harming farmers' feelings and interests."[13]

To carry out this kind of reform, however, central officials would have to gain firmer control over local officials. One way to facilitate reform of local governance has been to institute elections for village officials. Begun in 1999, such experiments in grassroots democracy have spread widely across China.[14] But the village officials up for election are not those with much real power over farmers' lives. Elected village officials who have dared to protest corruption and mismanagement of officials above them have sometimes been beaten or jailed.[15] Serious reform would require free elections for officials at the township and county levels of government. As yet, however, the government has not shown interest in this move, perhaps because it needs to retain minimal allegiance of most township and county officials in order to keep the lid on popular discontent, even as their behavior worsens such discontent.

Like a Third World colonial or neocolonial government unable to alleviate the sources of popular discontent, the current government can only maintain rural stability by keeping discontent fragmented. A major source of the fragmentation is the particularism of a social system based on familial relationships. In his study of Henan villages, Cao Jinqing notes that the importance of family and lineage power has increased since the economic reforms, with the consequence that mutual aid among villagers almost never goes beyond extended lineage groups. It is difficult for peasants to organize themselves on the basis of general, collective interests. Beyond the boundaries of family and clan, they "do not think about representing their own interests but look to someone else to represent their interests."[16]

As a consequence, although there have been thousands of local rural protests, these show no sign of linking up into widespread social movements. One way that such linkage might occur is through coalescence around ethnic or religious identities. Thus, angry Muslims (Hui) came together over considerable distances to protest an ethnic provocation in Shandong Province in fall 2000.[17] Similarly, thousands of mostly rural underground Catholics have protested government desecration of a pilgrimage site in Hebei.[18] The government devotes a disproportionate amount of energy to suppress such forces for rural solidarity. Another more modern practice that might contribute to such solidarity would be participation in democratic political campaigns for officials at levels higher than the village. It is not surprising that the government shows little interest in this. The government seems to be following the old adage that effective rule depends less on making the citizens love the government than on making sure that they do not love each other.

Theoretically, there could be two kinds of radical solutions to farmer discontent. One would be a return to Maoist-style socialism—redistribution of some urban resources to the rural sector, while maintaining restrictions on farmers' mobility from the countryside to the city. There is a surprising amount of support for this among farmers. Cao Jinqing, among other recent authors, notes that rural people continue to see Mao Zedong as their savior.[19] And when Gao Yijie, the doctor who has recently done much to expose the AIDS epidemic among villagers who have tried to supplement their incomes by selling their blood, visited a neglected, AIDS-stricken village in Henan (over the objections of local Party officials), a grateful recipient said, "I thank the Communist Party and I thank Chairman Mao."[20]

But there is virtually no support for Maoist socialism among national leaders. The alternative that is getting considerable support is a more radical liberalism. The well-connected sociologist Lu Xueyi writes:

> We need to create a unified market of one billion people. We can no longer continue with two divided markets in the city and the countryside and continue to lock peasants out of the cities. . . . Reform the present household registration system, open the doors to the cities and townships so as to open up peasant employment opportunities. . . . Naturally such a major change or transformation will need a set of laws and policies to put it into effect and would need to be implemented gradually. But making this change cannot be put off any longer. Maintaining the separation of the city and the countryside is unworkable.[21]

If farmers gained full property rights over their land and full residential mobility rights, they could liberate themselves from the traditional constraints of a peasant economy. They could make fuller, more efficient use of their labor power and they could pursue those fluid and voluntary relationships that are fundamental to modern civil society.

But there remain fundamental obstacles to this liberal solution for eliminating the barriers between city and countryside. There are the practical difficulties in establishing a single, unified market-based system in the Chinese hinterlands that lack adequate transportation and whose inhabitants lack the education necessary to make a transition to urban life. And there is a basic political difficulty. The influx of large numbers of farmers with full citizenship rights would be threatening to urban workers, who depend on cheap grain and are already angry about massive layoffs. As demonstrated by the Tiananmen movements of 1989, urban discontent has more of a potential than farmer discontent to coalesce into mass movements that could threaten the present regime. For the near future at least, a complete elimination of the barriers between city and countryside will probably be resisted by pragmatic, self-interested national leaders.

It may also be resisted for reasons of pure power politics. The logic of the present-day Chinese system is that the powerful make the weak bear the costs of economic development. Because they are disorganized, have few material resources, and have no effective representation at the national level, farmers have borne a disproportionate share of the costs.[22] The barriers separating city from countryside help consolidate the power of local rural officials as well as protect the power of urban officials, thereby ensuring that most of the costs of development will be borne by those at the bottom of each sector. But before we fully show how this works, we need to more completely describe socialist China and newly industrializing China.

Socialist China

In socialist China, social status has been dependent on rank within bureaucratic hierarchies. Power is acquired by being sponsored by superiors within the Communist Party. A satisfactory life course depends on joining a satisfactory "work unit," moving up its bureaucratic ranks, and finally retiring on a pension provided by the work unit. The system is justified by what Andrew Walder has called "neo-traditionalism," a system of organized dependency under political paternalism.[23] The basis of this social system has been the state-owned enterprises that were the foundation of the redistributionist, centrally planned socialist economy.

State-owned enterprises still employ about 40 percent of the Chinese urban workforce. The system, however, is now in crisis. Although state-owned enterprises are no longer micromanaged by central planning agencies, they are financed by loans through government banks that allocate money on the basis of political connections rather than economic efficiency. Having operated for years without pressure to turn a profit, so many of these enterprises are unable to pay back their loans that the Chinese banking system is probably technically bankrupt.

Most of the state-owned enterprises today are inefficient because they are bloated with workers. Although employing 40 percent of the urban workforce, they only produce less than 30 percent of the industrial output.

Under state socialism, full employment has been important because the state-owned enterprise has been responsible for the full range of social welfare benefits: housing, schooling, medical care, and pensions. In return for loyalty to the enterprises and to the political system that sustained them, workers were promised security.

But the enterprises can no longer keep this promise. They can no longer afford to pay for a full range of welfare benefits. Workers have to pay an ever larger deductible for medical care, for example, and pension benefits are now not enough to sustain a comfortable retirement. Yet for most workers there is no social security system that could provide affordable welfare benefits outside the "work units" that have employed them.[24]

To improve their efficiency, state-owned enterprises have been shedding workers. The process is usually called *xiagang*, or "stepping down." Workers lose most of their salary but are usually not evicted from the virtually free housing provided by the enterprise and they retain some access to medical benefits. Perhaps 45 million to 60 million urban workers have been laid off in this manner, and more will surely follow as China encounters the international market pressures brought to bear by membership in the World Trade Organization.[25] Many other state-owned enterprises are either being closed altogether or sold to private investors, sometimes in joint ventures with multinational corporations. When this happens, retired or redundant workers often lose all pension and welfare benefits.

In the early 1990s, many younger, entrepreneurial workers quit their jobs and, as the sayings went, "entered society" or "jumped into the sea" of free enterprise in the market economy. A "jumping into the sea fever" developed, based on the perception of abundant new opportunities in the private sector. By the mid-1990s, however, for many the opportunities seemed to have been an illusion. Most middle-aged workers (age 35 and above) found it impossible to find new jobs in the private sector, at least at the levels of income and benefits to which they had become accustomed. And retired workers have, at present, no replacement for the pensions lost when their former employers become privatized.[26]

With no exit from the state socialist system possible, unemployed workers are increasingly voicing their anger in public protests. There have been thousands of strikes and demonstrations, sometimes violent, throughout the old industrial areas of China since the mid-1990s. In 2001 and 2002, the protests seemed to be larger and somewhat more violent. In March 2002, for example, 50,000 workers staged several weeks of protests at the oil-production complex of Daqing in Heilongjiang Province—an enterprise hailed during the Maoist era as one of the heroic triumphs of Chinese socialism. The protests had to be brought under control by the People's Armed Police, China's paramilitary force for maintaining public order.[27] In this, as in other such protests, the workers' anger was ignited by the failure of the state-owned enterprise to maintain an adequate level of welfare and pension benefits for laid-off employees. Locked in a classic socialist system, the workers have not so much been demanding the end of socialism as they have been demanding that the system live up to its promises that it would provide them a decent level of social security in return for their loyalty.

Although it is obviously declining, the state socialist system is not smoothly dissolving into a market economy. It is imploding and crushing the hopes of many of those caught up in it. The final result could be large explosions of anger.

Newly Industrializing China

The source of China's current economic dynamism is its market-driven, export-oriented manufacturing system. In this system, status is based on money (and displayed through conspicuous consumption). Power depends on personal connections with bureaucrats (bought with money), but not on adherence to bureaucratic rules. A successful life course depends on getting enough money to take care of oneself. All of this is justified by a social Darwinist ideology of progress through competition. "Life is an ocean," as Karl Marx is reported to have said in an out-of-context quote in a Chinese tabloid, and "only those with a strong will can reach the other side."[28]

Newly industrializing China is a social, political, economic, and cultural system that generally follows the development model of Asian newly industrializing economies such as Taiwan, South Korea, Hong Kong, and Singapore. It is a model that uses the state to mobilize national labor and capital for manufacturing goods for export to the global consumer market—the center of which, of course, is the United States. As with other newly industrializing economies in the early stages of their development, the Chinese approach concentrates on using cheap labor to produce light industry products.[29]

At present much of Chinese export production comes from small factories in places like Shenzhen and Dongguan in Guangdong Province, and Xiamen in Fujian Province, where mostly young women workers turn out textiles, toys, and consumer electronics for less than ten cents per hour.[30]

But the sweatshops are giving way to higher-tech factories in places like Shanghai and Tianjin, where workers produce relatively advanced computer chips, mobile phones, and pharmaceuticals. The factories also employ white-collar workers for managing, accounting, and promotion. Much of China's emerging middle class comes from this stratum.

Much of the capital and technology for these factories come from abroad, and the products often end up being sold under the brand names of U.S., Japanese, South Korean, or Taiwanese companies. Capital flows in search of labor that is (1) relatively cheap for the amount of skill it requires and (2) flexible (i.e., it can be easily hired, fired, and moved around to meet the shifting needs of market-driven production). These economic requirements entail different kinds of social relations than are found in third-world China, with its farmers entangled in a web of kinship obligations, and in socialist China, with its organized dependence of workers on a managerial and political hierarchy. In areas where the newly industrializing economy is prevalent, the social milieu consists of loosely connected individuals. Order is maintained through authoritarian politics focused on keeping workers docile while allowing almost libertarian freedom to owners and managers. There is immediate police response at any sign of labor unrest, but little enforcement of worker safety or environmental protection regulations (where these exist at all).[31]

Such labor regimes were common in the early phases of many East Asian newly industrializing economies. However, there are important differences between China and the others. The latter were committed to steadily upgrading the quality of their national labor forces through education, so that they could produce more technology-intensive, value-added products. Thus, even if workers were suffering under harsh conditions, they could look forward to a better life for their children. But although the Chinese government wants to follow the lead of other newly industrializing economies in developing an economy based on high-tech production, it is not providing high-quality education for the children of most workers. Indeed, since most workers in the export-processing factories come from the countryside where schools have been steadily deteriorating, they might realistically expect that their children will get less education than they did. And when low-tech, semi-skilled jobs are replaced with high-tech, high-skilled occupations, the undereducated children of today's sweatshop workers may not qualify for the new jobs. Workers in the emerging Chinese high-tech industries will probably come from different labor pools—from graduates of schools in big cities or students returning from abroad.[32]

Another difference between the China development model and other East Asian newly industrializing economies is that the others usually were committed to industrial planning through which the government encouraged development of emerging new industries through strategic channeling of investment funds into research and development. The Chinese newly industrializing model is much more laissez faire. In comparison with the earlier phases of industrial development in Japan, South Korea, Taiwan, Hong Kong, and Singapore, there is a freewheeling, chaotic character to Chinese development.

To understand how newly industrializing China has been so successful, as well as to discern its potential failures, we now have to look at the relationships between newly industrializing China, socialist China, and third-world China.

Crossing Boundaries

The three institutionally and culturally incompatible social systems are interconnected through personal networks. The networks provide pathways through which certain groups of people can cross the boundaries between systems. The people carry with them important resources, mainly labor power and capital. Although the flow is not completely one way, most of the resources go into newly industrializing China. From socialist China it draws capital, and from third-world China, labor. The transfer is not carried out by any institutionalized, publicly legitimated process, but through individuals with the power to act independently of either modern law or traditional morality.

Thus, much of the startup capital for private industry in newly industrializing China has been appropriated by private individuals from the public property of state-owned enterprises—in a word, through corruption. But the term "corruption" is too broad to help us discern the many different ways in which this primitive capital accumulation takes place and to distinguish between the different degrees of harm and benefit brought about by these practices. Sociologists Ding Xueliang[33] and He Qinglian[34] have described in vivid detail the various methods—some very ingenious—in which private appropriation of public goods takes place. For example, the manager of a money-losing state-owned factory might form a private company that utilizes all of the best machinery and most skilled workers of the state-owned factory, and thus earns handsome profits in the market economy, some of which can be used to finance even further improvements in the private company. Meanwhile, the state-owned factory sinks deeper into debt and goes bankrupt. This and other schemes have a number of features in common: a manager who owes authority only to higher-level officials rather than to subordinate employees; high-level officials who enforce their authority not through formal rules but through personal, clientalistic relationships with subordinates; and unclear regulations for separating public and private interests. Some of these schemes amount to nothing less than, in the confession of one businessman who profited from them, "sucking the nation's blood."[35] But others, as suggested in the example cited here, might actually aid China's development by converting public assets to efficient use—and in a quicker, more effective way than if done through formal, bureaucratically approved procedures. Chinese economic development, however, is development of newly industrializing China, and it does not benefit workers who are unable to leave socialist China.

Although bureaucrats-turned-entrepreneurs can carry capital across the boundary between socialist China and newly industrializing China, they cannot usually leave socialist China completely behind. Their ability to acquire capital depends on their official position or at least their official connections. Since much of the appropriation of public property is officially illegal, they are always vulnerable to blackmail and must remain in the good graces of high officials for protection. In the absence of institutionalized contract laws, enforceable by impartial judges, capitalists also must rely on personal relationships with higher-level officials—or on criminal gangs that can only function effectively with permission from high-level officials—for protection of their interests.

Thus, the boundary between state and civil society begins to blur. The transition between state and civil society takes place in an "unofficial" realm, an informal, and usually partially hidden dimension of official bureaucracies, a realm that depends on bureaucratic structures even as it subverts them. There is really no good, established term to denote the political economy that results from this. Some scholars have called it "bureaucratic capitalism," but the term does not capture the anomic fluidity with which bureaucratic power is translated into capitalist wealth. Some have called it "relationship (*guanxi*) capitalism" to denote the extent to which it depends on informal, interpersonal relations. But that term does not capture the extent to which the relationships get their power through connections with established bureaucracies. Perhaps the best, although still imperfect, term might be "patrimonial capitalism." This captures the way in which powerful officials treat their organizations as their personal households and can make decisions without having to consistently follow rules.

In any case, the owners and investors of the dynamic enterprises in newly industrializing China do not (yet) form an independent bourgeoisie whose interests are at odds with the socialist state. Their interests would not lead to them toward any fundamental challenge to the current political arrangements that govern China.

If socialist China is the primary source of domestic capital (as opposed to foreign investment) for newly industrializing China, the primary source for labor is third-world China. About 150 million rural Chinese now belong to a "floating population" of migrant laborers. In Chinese, they are not called "workers," or *gongren*, which is the dignified name for the proletariat who were supposed to be the leaders and chief beneficiaries of the communist revolution. The rural migrants are simply said to "do labor"—*dagong*—and the term evokes the temporary, insecure, low-paid existence that they live. These laborers from the countryside have no permanent residence permits for the cities where they work. Some come on short-term contracts to work in export-oriented factories. But for most there is no possibility of finding careers in factory work. If they get too old or sick to work, or wish to get married, or become disabled, they are sent home to the countryside. Other migrant laborers come in illegally and are tolerated as long as there is a need for them to do jobs other urban residents do not want (and sometimes as long as appropriate bribes are paid to police and other officials). The men typically do low-skilled construction work and the women work as domestic servants. Some also fill jobs in the extensive underground economy, such as in the thriving prostitution industry. Migrant laborers are often looked down upon by urban residents and blamed (mostly unfairly) for rising crime and disorder. They can be arbitrarily sent back home when it appears that they might compete with urban residents for jobs, or even when authorities want to beautify a city—for example, when the International Olympic Committee visited Beijing to consider its bid to host the games.[36]

To get to the cities and find work, migrants usually have to rely on networks of informal brokers, often connected to power holders in their local towns and villages. Thus, movement out of the countryside is made possible only through the political authority structure of third-world China. Once in the cities, the migrants often have to rely on other unofficial brokers to negotiate relationships with the police and other urban authorities. Often they come without their spouses and they usually have to return home regularly to attend to family matters. They also may have to return for medical care, since they are not entitled to any in the city, as well as for scrutiny by local authorities, who remain responsible for guaranteeing their proper behavior. The unmarried housekeeper of an acquaintance in Beijing, for instance, had to return to her native village every six months to be examined for pregnancy (and to have an abortion if she were found pregnant).

Some migrants have become quite successful, especially by starting small retail businesses. Even those who have miserable jobs and low pay, however, continue to come to the cities, because the pay is more than they can get in the countryside. Much of their money is remitted back to their families to help pay off debts and perhaps to invest in local businesses. Also, as if in compensation for their low status in the cities, they sometimes build large houses back in their villages, or fancy tombs for their ancestors, a practice that uses up farmland and makes villagers even more dependent on income from labor migration.[37]

Both the money and the ideas that the migrants acquire are certainly bringing important changes to third-world China. The most visible signs of this urban influence are ubiquitous television sets and home appliances such as washing machines (which are popular even where there is no running water and they have to be filled by hand), and movie-star pinups (the modern rural aesthetic is partial to "bikini pictures," often of Western women). More important than the status symbols of consumer culture are the skills of commercial culture, which disseminate more slowly than consumer culture.[38] In some places, especially in suburban areas of Guangdong and Zhejiang, these influences are blurring the boundary between third-world China and newly industrializing China. Remittances from migrant workers help to finance township and village enterprises and the knowledge and contacts brought by returning migrant workers can make these enterprises successful.[39] However, as noted above, in many other areas of third-world China, especially farther inland, TVEs are collapsing, and rural industrialization is going backward.

As long as migrant workers do not have full rights of residence in cities, the fundamental boundaries between the social systems will remain in most places. Indeed, the very success of newly industrializing China, and the interests of the investors who most profit from it, depend on its difference vis-à-vis third-world China. It is that difference that ensures the constant supply of cheap and docile labor that is important for export-oriented development. The docility comes from the fact that miserable work in the newly industrializing system can bring relative status and prestige in the third-world system and that entrenched authorities in the third-world system—parents, clan leaders, local bosses—have an interest in disciplining the workers who go to the city. Although there has been much unrest directed against local power holders in the countryside, there has been little overt labor unrest in the export-oriented enclaves of newly industrializing China, even though the living conditions of laborers in this system are much worse than those of workers in the state-owned enterprises of socialist China.

Uneasy Balances

The uneasy balance among third-world China, socialist China, and newly industrializing China has so far maintained itself because almost everyone within these systems can have hope for some improvement in their lives by at least temporarily crossing the borders to another system. Underemployed farmers can improve their incomes by migrating to the cities; and they relieve themselves of their low status in the city by returning to flaunt their new money and their urban sophistication back home in the countryside. Modestly paid officials in urban bureaucracies and state-owned enterprises can turn their power into money by channeling investments into the newly industrializing system; and they can protect themselves against the uncertainties of cutthroat capitalist competition by relying on the political institutions of socialist China.

The biggest losers under the present arrangements are middle-aged workers in the system of state-owned enterprises who are losing their livelihoods but lack the skills necessary to find new work. Even they, however, are not totally without hope. At least sometimes, they can get connected to the more dynamically growing sectors of society through family members. Many urban families practice "one family, two systems." That is, one spouse works in the state sector (and makes full use of whatever entitlements to housing and health care that still exist there), and the other spouse or a son or daughter works in the newly industrializing sector—and not in the low-wage sector but in the relatively high-paid white-collar sectors. The spouse or children can then make up for other spouse's lost wages and pension benefits. And as China makes the transition from being a manufacturer of commodities made with low-cost, semi-skilled labor to manufacturer of high-tech products, the people who find jobs in the newly industrializing sector will be from the families of workers in today's distressed state-owned enterprises. The one-family, two-systems solution may not work in many cases, however, because of the success of the government in enforcing its one-child policy in the cities. An adult singleton now has to take care of both his or her own parents and in-laws. Together with an increasing divorce rate, this means that urban family members will find it more difficult to compensate for the losses some members face in the changing economic system.

In the near future, at least, the most volatile sector of Chinese society will probably be its urban working class, angry and desperate because of the implosion of state-owned enterprises. The urban working class has so far shown itself unable to develop enough solidarity to overturn the status quo. It is divided internally because of the nature of work units in state-owned enterprises. By providing a total package of services for workers, and by restricting lateral movement of workers to other enterprises, these work units kept workers from developing the habit of linking up with counterparts in other factories or industrial sectors. Moreover, as we have pointed out, the urban proletariat is not inclined to link up with laborers migrating from rural China and it has little sympathy for farmers in general. The Chinese government is extremely sensitive toward groups that might bridge these divisions among the discontented. It crushes any attempts to form autonomous labor unions. And the vigor of its persecution of the Falun Gong and similar religious groups is probably due to fear of the capacity of such groups to forge bonds across regions and social classes.[40] For all that, it appears that workers are beginning to link up with aggrieved counterparts throughout China. The stability of the current regime will depend on how successful they are.

Consequences

China today is thus an unstable condominium of at least three different social systems. For now, what ties them together is codependency without synergy—a situation in which it is in the interest of the most powerful people in each system to maintain a status quo that exploits the weakest people within each system. This is a situation so complex, and potentially so unstable, that there is no way to accurately forecast its future.

To hold this fragile unity of complex parts together, the Chinese Communist Party has been reinventing itself, first in practice and now in theory, as a corporatist party, that is, a party that supposedly represents the interests of all sectors of society and reconciles competing interests through negotiations among elites from each sector. Jiang Zemin's theory of the "Three Represents," which was made official Party doctrine at the 16th Party Congress, states that the Party represents all advanced progressive forces in Chinese society, including business entrepreneurs, who are now officially eligible to become Party members. If one were to represent this symbolically, the hammer and sickle might have to be superimposed on top of a stock portfolio! How are these interests—fundamentally incompatible in classical Marxist theory—to be reconciled? Jiang Zemin's theory is mainly a pastiche of empty slogans that give no coherent answer. In practice, however, the interests are being reconciled through the dynamics of a patrimonial state. Not bound to the masses through enforceable bureaucratic rules, the elites bind themselves to one another through webs of personal, clientalistic relationships. Their main common denominator is an interest in maintaining the Party's monopoly on rule.

Such a corporatist party conjoined with a patrimonial state can maintain a reasonable degree of social stability and economic development for a long time—a good example would be Mexico's Institutional Revolutionary Party, which governed Mexico for seventy-one years. A problem endemic to such political arrangements, however, is corruption. Irregular behavior is built into the very process of maintaining peace through personal negotiations among elites who nominally represent different interests. The Party's monopoly on power further increases such temptations. A strong sense of nationalism may temporarily maintain some degree of integrity among Party personnel. But the temptations of easy money proffered by modern criminal groups—smugglers, narco traffickers, and money launderers—quickly and deeply undermine such elite integrity and cohesion as well as deepening the anger and cynicism of citizens toward their government. Citizen disgust with such corruption led to the peaceful demise of the Mexican PRI and the Kuomintang in Taiwan, which were swept aside at the ballot box. Might the same happen to the CCP in China?

In the above-cited cases, the peaceful demise of corrupt party structures required, first of all, the establishment of formal procedures for democratic elections, even though the ruling party regularly used its power to subvert the formal rules. The Chinese government is now beginning to develop such rules for free elections at the rural level, even though, as we have seen, the rules are regularly broken so that the Party can retain its dominance. Although there are no signs that this will happen in the near future, one could imagine a scenario in which to co-opt discontented citizens, the government allowed such elections at higher levels. Even if it did, the

Party would still probably retain all of the effective levers of power. What could finally break that power would be the growth of an active civil society among those social sectors who do not have a stake in continued corruption and who have the sophistication and organizational skills to make use of the formal rules to pursue their interests in a peaceful manner.

We can do no more than speculate about how and when such an active civil society might arise. The most probable source would be the emerging middle classes described at the beginning of this chapter. Millions of people now engage in the technical, managerial, and public relations work of the emerging private sector. Imbued with a sense that they can get ahead on the basis of their own talents, adept at new modes of communication like the Internet, accustomed to constructing identities on the basis of free choice among consumer goods, able to interact with like-minded peers on the basis of nonpolitical horizontal relationships that flourish in an expanding private sphere, such citizens are beginning to develop an array of nonpolitical free associations devoted to self-help, education, and charitable endeavors. According to Deborah Davis, we should not underestimate "the ability of increased sociability in nonofficial activities to incubate loyalties that ultimately generate the actions capable of weakening or toppling an authoritarian state."[41]

But the foundations for such a civil society are only located in one relatively small section of newly industrializing China. It may take several decades before it flourishes to the point where it could generate alternatives to the current authoritarian rule. Even this presupposes a China that remains stable and continues on a path of steady economic growth.

The uneasy balance of contradictory forces that I have described in terms of "one country, three systems" is, then, inherently unstable. Its evolution will probably take place not according to some predictable dialectic but according to the contingencies of chaos theory, in which small changes in one area can lead unpredictably to big changes in another. In such an open-ended situation, the quality of leadership can make a big difference, which is why the decisions made at the 16th Party Congress may be so important.

Notes

1. Hanlong Lu, "To Be Relatively Comfortable in an Egalitarian Society," in *The Consumer Revolution in Urban China*, ed. Deborah S. Davis (Berkeley: University of California Press, 2000), 124–141.

2. Deborah S. Davis, "Introduction: A Revolution in Consumption," in *The Consumer Revolution in Urban China*, ed. Davis (Berkeley: University of California Press, 2000), 1–22.

3. The term is borrowed from popular psychology to denote a relationship that is in part mutually harmful, even as it provides partners with certain satisfactions that neither is willing to forgo. I use it in contrast with a genuinely, mutually beneficial interdependence.

4. This terminology was originally suggested to me by Chalmers Johnson.

5. William L. Parish and Martin King Whyte, *Village and Family in Contemporary China* (Chicago: University of Chicago Press, 1978).

6. Richard Madsen, *Morality and Power in a Chinese Village* (Berkeley: University of California Press, 1984).

7. Cao Jinqing, *Huanghebiande Zhongguo: Yige Xuezhe dui Xiangcun Shehui de Guancha yu Sikao* [China Along the Yellow River: A Scholar's Observations and Meditations on Chinese Rural Society] (Shanghai: Wenyi Chuban She, 2000). For this essay, I am using the English summaries provided by David Cowhig, available at www.usembassy-china.org.cn/english/sandt/china-along-yellow-river.htm, accessed on July 1, 2002.

8. For analysis of growth from 1988 to 1993, see Christopher S.P. Tong, "Total Factor Productivity Growth and Its Spatial Disparity across China's Township and Village Enterprises," *Journal of Contemporary China* 10, no. 26 (2001): 155–171. For a journalistic account of the recent collapse, see Jasper Becker, *The Chinese* (New York: Free Press, 2000).

9. Jinqing, *China Along the Yellow River*, Cowhig summary (see n. 7).

10. Ibid.

11. *Nanfang Zhoumo*, August 25, 2000, available at www.nanfangdaily.com.cn, accessed on August 27, 2000; Li Changpin, *Wo Xiang Zongli Shno Shihua* [Tell Truth to the Premier] (Beijing: Guanming Ribao Chubanshe, 2001), 20–27.

12. Willy Wo-Lap Lam, "Rural Discontent Mounts," *South China Morning Post*, February 9, 2000, p. 13.

13. *People's Daily*, January 8, 2002, p. 1.

14. Tianjian Shi, "Cultural Values and Democracy in the People's Republic of China," *China Quarterly* 162 (2000): 540–559.

15. For just one recent example reported in the Western press, see Erik Eckholm, "China's Party Bosses Thwart Local Leaders," *New York Times*, April 25, 2002.

16. Jinqing, *China Along the Yellow River*, Cowhig summary (see n. 7). See also, Jiang Changyun, "Rural Land and Social Security for Farmers," *Da Gong Bao* (Hong Kong), March 9, 2002 (Foreign Broadcast Information Service translation, March 15, 2002).

17. This incident happened in Yangxin County, Shandong Province, during November 2000. The demonstration was provoked by the hanging of a pig's head in front of a local mosque. "News of the incident prompted Huis from elsewhere in China to travel to Yangxin in a show of support, leading to three large clashes between Huis and police in November." See "Chinese Police Fire on Muslim Demonstrators, Kill Five," *Associated Press* (Beijing), December 15, 2000, available at www.ap.org, accessed on December 15, 2000.

18. Richard Madsen, *China's Catholics: Tragedy and Hope in an Emerging Civil Society* (Berkeley: University of California Press, 1998), 90–93.

19. Jinqing, *China Along the Yellow River*, Cowhig summary (see n. 7).

20. Gao Yaojie, "My AIDS Prevention Journey," trans. David Cowhig; Chinese original available at www.aizhi.org/jkwz/journey/htm, accessed on June 5, 2001.

21. Lu Xueyi, "The Peasants Are Suffering, The Villages Are Very Poor," *Dushu*, January 2001. Translation by David Cowhig, available at www.usembassy-china.org.cn/english/sandt/villages.html, accessed on April 23, 2001.

22. The most vulnerable farmers bear more of the burden. Among the most vulnerable are women. The rate of suicide among Chinese rural women is among the highest in the world. Unlike most other societies, where women commit suicide less frequently than men, the rate for Chinese women is sharply higher than that of rural men. See Michael Phillips et al., "Suicide Rates in China, 1995–99," *Lancet* 359, no. 9309 (2002): "Among young adults 15–34 years of age, suicide was the leading cause of death, accounting for 19% of all deaths. The rate in women was 25% higher than in men, mainly because of the large number of suicides in young rural women. Rural rates were three times higher than urban rates—a difference that remained true for both sexes, for all age groups, and over time." See also Paul G. Pickowicz and Liping Wang, "Village Voices, Urban Activists: Women, Violence, and Gender Inequality in Rural China," in *Popular China: Unofficial Culture in a Globalizing Society*, ed. Perry Link, Richard P. Madsen, and Paul G. Pickowicz (Lanham, Md.: Rowman & Littlefield, 2002), 57–87.

23. Andrew G. Walder, *Communist Neo-Traditionalism: Work and Authority in Chinese Industry* (Berkeley: University of California Press, 1986).

24. World Bank, "China Pension Reform of State Run Enterprises," Report no. 15121-CHA, August 22, 1996, as cited in Becker, *The Chinese*, 40.

25. Dorothy J. Solinger "WTO and China's Workers," *China Enters the WTO: The Death Knell for State-Owned Enterprises?* ed. Gang Lin, *Asia Program Special Report* 103 (Washington, D.C.: Woodrow Wilson International Center for Scholars, June 2002), 3.

26. Ibid., 4–5.

27. Lynn O'Donnell, "Armed Police to Break Standoff," *The Australian*, March 20, 2002, available at www.theaustralian.news.com.au, accessed on March 20, 2002.

28. Quoted in Yuezhi Zhao, "The Rich, the Laid Off, and the Criminal in Tabloid Tales: Read All About It!" in *Popular China: Unofficial Culture in a Globalizing Society*, ed. Perry Link, Richard P. Madsen, and Paul G. Pickowicz (Lanham, Md.: Rowman & Littlefield, 2002), 124.

29. Ezra F. Vogel, *One Step Ahead in China: Guangdong under Reform* (Cambridge, Mass.: Harvard University Press, 1989), 426–449.

30. Anita Chan, "The Culture of Survival: Lives of Migrant Women through the Prism of Private Letters," in *Popular China: Unofficial Culture in a Globalizing Society*, ed. Perry Link, Richard P. Madsen, and Paul G. Pickowicz (Lanham, Md.: Rowman & Littlefield, 2002), 163–188.

31. For a comprehensive account, see Chan, "The Culture of Survival."

32. Fei-ling Wang, "Floaters, Moonlighters, and the Underemployed: A National Labor Market with Chinese Characteristics," *Journal of Contemporary China* 7, no. 19 (1998): 459–475.

33. Xueliang Ding, "The Informal Asset Stripping of Chinese State Firms," *The China Journal* 43 (2000): 1–28; Ding, "Informal Privatization through Internationalization," *British Journal of Political Science* 30, no. 1 (2000); Ding, "Systemic Irregularity and Spontaneous Property Transformation in the Chinese Financial Sector," *The China Quarterly* 163, no. 1 (2000): 655–676; Ding, "The Quasi-Criminalization of a Business Sector in China: Deconstructing the Construction Sector Syndrome," *Crime, Law, and Social Change* 35, no. 3 (2001): 177–201.

34. He Qinglian, *Xiandaihuade Xianjing* [Pitfalls of Modernization] (Beijing: Jinri Zhongguo Chubanshe, 1998).

35. Quoted in Ding, "Informal Privatization," 137.

36. Li Zhang, *Strangers in the City: Reconfiguration of Space, Power, and Social Networks within China's Floating Population* (Stanford, Calif.: Stanford University Press, 2001).

37. Zhong Dajun, "China's Error: Adverse Impacts of China's Common Land System and Household Registration System on its Land Resources," *Guangzhou Xin Jingji*, March 20, 2001 (Foreign Broadcast Information Service translation). This article describes the deleterious effects on the natural environment due to wasteful spending on big tombs by newly rich farmers.

38. Jinqing, *China Along the Yellow River*, Cowhig summary (see n. 7).

39. Rachel Murphy, "Return Migration, Entrepreneurship and Local State Corporatism in Rural China: The Experience of Two Counties in South Jiangxi," *Journal of Contemporary China* 9, no. 24 (2000): 231–247.

40. Human Rights Watch, *Dangerous Meditation: China's Campaign against Falungong* (N.Y.: Human Rights Watch, 2002).

41. Davis, "Introduction," 21.

Chapter 5

New Leaders, New Foreign Policymaking Procedures?

David Bachman

The leadership transition expected over the next several years in China will have important implications for Chinese foreign policy. At the time of this writing, it remains unclear how the succession process is working out. There was little apparent controversy during the 16th National Congress of the Chinese Communist Party (CCP), the first stage of the succession when the third generation of leaders with Jiang Zemin at its core nominally began to cede power to the fourth generation, with Hu Jintao as its top-ranking leader. Yet up to the day of its conclusion and appointment of new Party leadership bodies, rumors abounded that there were ongoing fights and squabbles among the leadership about the top lineup. Moreover, for the first time in the history of the study of elite politics in China, source material that was assumed to be from the dossiers of those to be promoted made its way out of China. According to the English-language summary of these archives, the dynamics of the succession were, for the most part, re-solved months previously. However, the leadership lineup presented in this material differed significantly from the final outcome. According to this source, based on Party materials, the Politburo Standing Committee was to be made up of seven individuals, one of whom was supposed to be Li Ruihuan. The actual results differed significantly, as there were nine members of the Politburo Standing Committee, and Li, who was expected to occupy the number-two position in the Party, did not make it into the Politburo Standing Committee. There were other discrepancies between the internal material and the actual results as well.[1] Do these differences fundamentally negate the conclusions drawn by Andrew J. Nathan and Bruce Gilley in *China's New Rulers: The Secret Files*, meaning that the struggle over succession remains ongoing, or are the actual results indicative of marginal changes in a basically scripted result? Arguments can be advanced for either point of view (and Nathan and Gilley concede that their analysis was provisional, and that actual last-minute politicking could alter their reading of leadership positions and numbers). What has indisputably emerged is that Jiang Zemin retains substantial authority within China—he remains chair of the Central Military Commission (CMC) and president of the People's Republic of China (PRC), at least until March 2003. Whether he retains his chairmanship of the CMC is one of the big unanswered questions, with important implications for leadership issues, political power, and perhaps for Chinese foreign policy. Furthermore, the possibility that the succession and leadership lineup remains unsettled leaves open the question of whether foreign policy will become an arena of leadership and succession struggle. Thus, a great deal of uncertainty continues to surround leadership issues in China, and how others view Chinese politics, with significant spillover possibilities for Chinese foreign policy.

The most important potential impact of efforts to continue to contest the succession arrangements is to raise the possibility of much greater struggles for power within the elite. Trust will decline within the elite, and established procedures or norms will not be seen as binding. Consensus building and the establishment of credible commitments will be extremely difficult. Policies, policymaking arenas, and appointments may become areas of intense political struggle, diminishing the likelihood of sound procedures and well-developed policies—in domestic and foreign affairs.

While the domestic leadership transition (however it is resolved) is taking place, major changes are occurring simultaneously in the international system and in China's relationship with the international system. Particularly in light of September 11, and an emerging "post–Cold War" foreign policy of the United States, China's leaders wonder (as do many others) about the shape, dimensions, norms, and rules of this potential new international order. Even as the international order appears to be on the crux of major change and transformation, the effects of Chinese accession to the World Trade Organization (WTO) are just beginning to ramify throughout the Chinese governing apparatus and society. If implemented as written, China's WTO accession fundamentally compromises elements of Chinese sovereignty under CCP rule to an unprecedented degree, and exposes China much more thoroughly to international market trends, rules, and regulations. In short, China's leadership transition is occurring at a time of great uncertainty about the direction of the international system generally and China's role within it specifically. It is trite but true to say that this combination of factors is both a great challenge and a potential opportunity for China's new leaders.

When Do Domestic Institutions Matter?

A critical issue in assessing domestic foreign policy institutions of any nation-state is whether they matter. This is not to say they are unimportant; after all, in most cases some institutional processes collect information, analyze it, make recommendations to policymakers, implement the decision-makers' policy choices, and monitor the effects of the policy, generating new or more information and so on. For those who argue for the salience of an approach emphasizing the domestic sources of foreign policy, it becomes essential to identify how and why the particular decision-making system, or institutions at the heart of the foreign policymaking apparatus, matter. Asking this question and answering that the domestic institutions matter imply that such an approach provides answers that deviate from other approaches or run counter to expectations. Domestic institutions would matter in China's leadership change if there were significant changes in Chinese foreign policy behavior. They would also matter if international systemic models of foreign policy behavior could not explain or explain well Chinese foreign policy behavior. (Similarly, a focus on Hu Jintao as the presumed core of the next generation of leadership, and his likely role as the ultimate foreign-policy decision-maker should show that his decisions are likely to differ in important ways from the types of decisions that Jiang Zemin would have made, or more generally, that Hu's choices might differ from those of any reasonable, rational individual.[2]) Studies of foreign policy decision-making apparatuses and institutions are useful descriptively, but they carry much greater analytical weight when they produce findings that challenge existing expectations, theories, or patterns.

Because Hu Jintao and the fourth generation of leaders have not yet held the highest positions in the Chinese party-state, it is impossible to argue that they as leaders, or the foreign policy institutions and norms that they may establish, will matter.[3] But there are a number of reasons why I believe that it is likely they will.

First, as noted above, the nature of the international system's operation may have changed fundamentally since September 11. The Bush administration has undertaken actions and begun to articulate a new post–Cold War foreign policy for the United States that breaks with many elements of U.S. foreign policy, existing in some cases since the earliest days after World War II. The reasons why the United States appears to be altering the rules of the international game (at least for itself) are beside the point here, but the changes themselves are important, and because they are still evolving, they remain uncodified. This increases the importance of how others perceive U.S. words and deeds. If the United States is truly articulating a new stance toward the world, the rest of the world will pay attention to the world's only superpower (or hyperpower as some intellectuals call it). Since the U.S. stance is only nascent, there are not a lot of precedents on which to calculate or project future U.S. behavior. U.S. standard operating procedures are still emerging to manage this new U.S. relationship with the international system and the rest of the world, and while these remain undefined, the rest of the world can only guess about what this new posture means in terms of institutions, norms, and practices.

In recent months, the Bush administration has terminated the Anti-Ballistic Missile (ABM) Treaty, and promised to build a ballistic-missile defense system. It has suggested that it will initiate the use of force when the U.S. leadership determines that weapons of mass destruction are under development in some countries (presumably in the case of undeclared nuclear powers). It has shown a distinct lack of enthusiasm for multilateral institutions, particularly within the United Nations framework (such as the Kyoto Convention on global warming and the International Criminal Court). Its actions with regard to protecting the domestic steel industry and supporting greatly expanded agricultural production subsidies, among others, may imperil future rounds of trade liberalization under the WTO, and perhaps the WTO itself. The U.S. defense build-up will further widen the gap between the defense capabilities of the United States and all other nation-states. General U.S. economic strength and high-technology capabilities suggest that it will be a very long time before the United States might be faced with a true peer competitor. In the meantime, at least for the Bush administration, a much more unilateralist United States, less concerned with the international public good, seems to be emerging.

Structural realist theories of international relations[4] suggest that in such circumstances, other states will either have to bandwagon (follow the U.S. lead, appease the United States, and so on) or balance as part of an international coalition, and/or build up their own resources so that they can defend their interests. Structural realist explanations are most interested in the questions of war and peace, and do not claim to explain the specific foreign policy of any state. But these theorists would argue that given the imbalance of power between the United States and China or between the United States and a coalition including China, that China should bandwagon or appease the United States.

It seems clear that for quite some time, China has been both going along with the United States on some issues, particularly the war on terrorism and muting the confrontation with Taiwan, while on other issues, China is trying to balance against the United States. China continues to develop its military forces. The termination of the ABM treaty and moves to build a U.S. missile defense will likely accelerate the build-up of China's strategic forces. China in the meantime has sought to strengthen its bilateral relations with Russia and the European Union, and sought to advance a number of more collective initiatives, such as free trade with the Association for Southeast Asian Nations.

The fact that China seems able to pick and choose between bandwagoning and balancing strategies suggests that structural realist theory is sufficiently indeterminate for explaining Chinese foreign policy in the near future. If theories cast at the level of the international system do not fully explain China's behavior, then perhaps theories that are less general and more specific, including those focused on Chinese domestic institutions, might. In particular, theories focusing on international and domestic interactions and linkages may be particularly useful.

In terms of these linkages, China's recent accession to the WTO symbolizes a new relationship between China and the world. Put simply, China must conform to international rules and norms concerning trade, services, intellectual property, and investment to varying degrees. China's failure to conform to the international rules of the game can lead it to be sanctioned by the WTO and its member economies. As China becomes an ever-larger trading nation (sixth largest in 2001) and the second-largest recipient of direct foreign investment, the ties of the international economy seem to bind China more firmly to the workings of international institutions and norms.

China's rapidly growing stake in the global economy, and more generally international stability, is a constraint on the Chinese government's freedom of action. But China's expanding role in the international economy and its WTO membership have given China new tools to use in its international economic policy. Already China has made its voice heard within the WTO, apparently successfully limiting some of the influence of the major developed trading nations in the WTO.[5] Contrary to general expectations, the PRC has brought more cases to the WTO about U.S. trade restrictions (on steel) than the United States has brought to the WTO about Chinese trade restrictions. (However, the United States seems to be continuing with a policy of quiet bilateral diplomacy to handle trade issues with China.) Even the threat that WTO market liberalization poses to China's state-owned enterprises seems to have worked out contrary to previous expectations in the case of the automobile industry, one of China's heretofore most protected and inefficient sectors. Major international automakers are competing for the Chinese market. Given limited, but growing consumer purchasing power, foreign manufacturers need to compete on the basis of price. Thus, they rely on an expanding array of Chinese auto parts producers. Chinese corporations are now putting these parts together in "domestic" cars that are beginning to erode foreign market share.[6]

The point here is not that China is unconstrained by the workings of the international economy (or other international regimes) and its norms and institutions. Rather, China seems to have been remarkably successful thus far in gaining a great deal from the international system at relatively low cost to its autonomy and sovereignty. Indeed, commentators are just beginning to recognize how the development of China as a major production base for multinational products increases the vulnerability of developed nations.[7]

The international system constrains the Chinese government's range of foreign policy choices. It appears, however, that the constraints are not immutable, they may not reinforce each other, and the constraints are not so tight as to prevent Chinese leaders from having some room for maneuver within existing international institutions, norms, and practices. This maneuvering room may be large or small, and the ultimate choice may largely reinforce prevailing institutional practices. But the fact that there was a set of realistic alternative policy choices argues for an examination of the Chinese institutional and leadership context for Chinese foreign policymaking.

Succession and Foreign Policy

If the CCP is to remain in power, China's new leadership, however constituted, faces a number of imperatives. Many of these imperatives are not all that different from those of most other governments. It must collect taxes, maintain basic law and order (social stability), promote economic growth, and provide for national defense. More particular to China is to continue economic system reform and transition, and the development of at least urban welfare systems that facilitate economic reform and social stability, if they are adequately funded. China's new leaders must at least pay lip service to the issue of China–Taiwan reunification and socialist ideology. Taiwan cannot become internationally recognized as an independent state during the new leadership's watch without grave political repercussions. The leadership must continue to do things that are likely to enhance the limited legitimacy of CCP rule—appear to crack down on corruption, promote Chinese nationalism, increase China's international presence in a positive way, diminish or at least stabilize the growing inequalities throughout China, and make Party rule more efficient. This may not exhaust the list of things the leaders must do (e.g., begin to improve air and water quality, and improve the environment more generally). All of the above, needless to say, are complex problems, affecting many political interests in China. They can be broken down into further subcategories (e.g., banking reform) that are also extremely complex, and which may defy easy or quick solutions.

Coupled with limited legitimacy and power, the new leadership is highly unlikely to undertake dramatic new initiatives to cope with these and other problems. Incrementalism, at least until power is consolidated by the fourth generation, is likely to have been the hallmark of the new leadership. However, should Jiang Zemin or others interfere, and at least temporarily prevail, a more disjointed style of policymaking might prevail, as the institutions of decision making become loci for the struggle for power. Any decision made and any policy implemented could become a club to be used in the power struggle, either demonstrating the skill and quality of those making the decision or proving the reverse. One can imagine this kind of circumstance leading to three different types of outcomes: paralysis, for fear of making mistakes that can incur attacks by others; incrementalism (or simply maintaining existing policies) so that there is less to be criticized; or a high-risk, high-potential–reward strategy—if one is going to be vulnerable, go all out for a high payoff. Unfortunately, there is no way to predict accurately what decision set will be chosen.

If Jiang fully retires within a short period of time (which, as will be discussed below, seems relatively unlikely), the decision-making system, biased as it is toward incrementalism, will have that tendency reinforced by the inevitable politicking taking place within the new leadership. In addition to the ongoing jockeying for standing, status, and influence within the leadership, there are significant differences among the new leaders on basic attitudes toward reform and other fundamental issues. None of the new leaders opposes the reform policies to date. But there are major differences on whether to push further reforms through rapidly, or whether to emphasize social stability. Other elements of personal and political style will have to be worked out within the new leadership. Because of the relative inexperience of most new leaders in foreign affairs, and the unified acceptance of the idea of the importance of a peaceful international environment for China's domestic development, it is unlikely that Chinese foreign policy will significantly depart from its current line, assuming that political conflicts within the leadership are reasonably managed.

However, it is well known that there are not particularly strong ties between Jiang and Hu Jintao (this is not to say that there are negative ties between the two). It is also thought that Jiang is not entirely reconciled to giving up all his power and perquisites in 2003.[8] This creates a situation where Jiang may be tempted to use his supporters (the "Shanghai faction" including Huang Ju, Zeng Qinghong, and Wu Bangguo, and also Jia Qinglin and Li Changchun) to limit, constrain, or if need be conspire against Hu Jintao. This possibility creates a possibly very dangerous situation, and there are strong CCP norms inhibiting overt factional conflict at the highest level. Under such circumstances, we can speculate about what the various actors in the leadership might try to do and what sort of results are likely to come of their interactions.

Hu Jintao, with limited political clout, and a desire to consolidate power without alienating potential allies and further solidifying the opposition of his rivals, would try to avoid hard decisions that impose costs on China (and key interests in China). He would try to diffuse responsibility for difficult decisions, try to structure issues in ways that on patronage and personnel issues, he has the key say, but on issues where decisions must be made and costs are high, he would try to incorporate everyone, and generally build a consensus. Such a deliberate politically calculated style also seems to fit his personality.[9] He would not boldly assert prerogatives, especially vis-à-vis Jiang Zemin and the People's Liberation Army (PLA). While trying to expand his network of loyal supporters within the elite, he would not pursue or target Jiang's followers for attack, unless they were clearly and massively linked to some scandal. In short, Hu's strategy is likely to be one in which he tries to build up his political capital over a period of several years. This would require him to continue to support Chinese nationalism, at least rhetorically, maintain the build-up of the PLA, manage PRC–Taiwan and PRC–U.S. relations, and travel and meet with foreign leaders extensively. He will try to build consensus within the leadership, if only to try to minimize his personal responsibility. One of his greatest assets can be that he is the face of China internationally, and no competitor for power or rival, even Jiang Zemin, can substitute for Hu's official role as China's leader.

Assuming that Jiang Zemin wishes to remain the key leader in China despite his retirement from a number of his top positions, his strategy is likely to be to try to hold on to at least one of his official positions, most likely chairman of the CMC, and to several of the top foreign policy positions that do not clearly attach to any particular office, which he now holds. In particular, these are the Foreign Affairs Leadership Small Group (FALSG) and the Taiwan Affairs Leadership Small Group (more about these small groups below). He might push hard for one of his protégés to be vice premier, without going so far as to egregiously violate Party norms. He is likely to acquiesce to Hu's elevation, but he will try to circumscribe Hu's position as much as possible. Jiang's age and declining vigor will work against him. Pressure will grow in the Party for him to be less active, and it is far from clear what "long-term" goals he can pursue. Clearly he wishes to be well regarded in PRC history, and he seems to desire to pull the strings of personnel and key policy issues for at least a while longer.[10] These two goals may contradict each other, and his legitimacy to intervene on personnel and policy issues will diminish after his retirement from top Party and government positions.

Assuming that one, if not all, of Jiang's protégés in the fourth generation wish to be the top leader in China, they must appear to be accepting of Hu's elevation and cooperating with him, while at the same time trying to maneuver him into having to make controversial and difficult decisions. Arguably, they have an interest in forcing Hu to make nonincremental decisions, believing that they will not work as intended, or if they do, the short-term costs of the decisions will become apparent much more quickly than will the potential long-term benefits in such areas as banking and fiscal reform, further economic reform more generally, and perhaps even in the area of political reform. Raising the pressure on the Taiwan issue, or exacerbating U.S.–China differences might also be issues over which they can pressure Hu. (But stratagems involving Taiwan and the United States could be very dangerous to those who might attempt to manipulate these issues.) In other words, they want to force issues on Hu and make him take the responsibility, assuming that Hu's decisions will cause as many or more problems than they solve. And as long as the "Shanghai faction" holds major positions in the new leadership, they will be in position to subtly sabotage Hu's positions.

But Jiang's followers are faced with the difficult task of maintaining solidarity, so that they can work collectively and not be subject to divide-and-rule tactics by Hu (and the non-Jiang faction leaders in the new leadership). One way to do this is to reach an understanding on the division of positions should they topple Hu. But such a compact may not be stable. It will clearly violate Party norms on leadership and factionalism. Moreover, given clear public commitments to stability and unity within the country and within the Party, initiating attacks on Hu is highly risky. The better strategy is to put him in a position where he fails, or proves to be not up to the challenges of being the "core" of the fourth generation of leaders.

Other political figures will be involved in the political infighting related to Hu's elevation and attempts to consolidate power. These would include other members of the third generation who might have a particular stake in succession, policy issues, or their own position in retirement, such as Li Peng, Zhu Rongji, and Li Ruihuan; non–Jiang-connected, fourth-generation leaders, especially Wen Jiabo, and perhaps top-ranking military leaders. The permutations and interactions become extremely complex when additional personnel become involved in trying to extrapolate how the competing individual interests in leadership succession will play themselves out, and how this will affect China's foreign policy.

From the perspectives of Hu, Jiang, and the "Shanghai faction," it seems likely to me that there will be a strong bias in the near term to maintain the status quo as it existed in the last years of the Jiang period. It is hard for Jiang to be unhappy with that, and makes it hard for his followers to complain as well. This gives Hu time to build up his position, and see Jiang gradually weakening. Obviously, leaders respond to events at least as much as they initiate them, and it is impossible to predict what international or internal developments will require decisions from the Chinese leadership. But to the extent that exogenous developments are limited over the next few years, it is unlikely that there will be broad foreign policy departures (from the previous positions) under the fourth generation of leaders. As noted, however, Hu may spend a great deal of time traveling, trying to arrange summits and state visits that highlight his leading role and his position as China's internationally recognized leader.

Historically, it is hard to argue that foreign policy was a critical issue in succession politics and major power struggles. Under Mao, elements of foreign policy developments were part of the rhetoric associated with succession and power struggles, but it is far from clear that they were significant.[11] Criticisms of foreign policy were implied in the purge of Liu Shaoqi in the Cultural Revolution, and certainly Mao's concern that Liu might lead China in the direction of "Soviet-style revisionism" was a powerful impetus to the Cultural Revolution and Liu's persecution. But this had less to do with the specifics of foreign policy, where Liu's role was limited, than with Mao's own idiosyncratic and evolving definition of "true socialism." It also used to be argued that Lin Biao's fall in 1971 was connected to foreign policy issues, especially policies toward the superpowers, but recent scholarship has cast profound doubt on such views. The Gang of Four used China's expanded foreign trade and Zhou Enlai's and Deng Xiaoping's willingness to trade Chinese oil for technology and factories as part of its repertoire of criticisms of veteran leaders, but these issues were not at the core of their attacks on them, or their defense of the Cultural Revolution.[12] Indeed, reflective of Mao's dominance of the policy processes, there is little evidence of sustained, major conflicts on foreign policy issues while he was alive.

During the Hua Guofeng interregnum, foreign policy issues seemed to be a factor to some extent, but Deng's replacing Hua had much more to do with the legacies of the Cultural Revolution than it did with foreign policy. And the post-1980 veiled criticisms of Hua do not suggest he opposed normalization of relations with the United States, over which Deng had personal charge.

Under Deng, the connection between foreign policy and power issues is even less evident. The reason for this is clear—Deng had ultimate say in foreign policy from 1978 to some time in the early 1990s. Hu Yaobang and Zhao Ziyang were removed from power because they would not suppress student protests, among other perceived domestic failings. Only in the 1989 to 1991 period do major disputes over foreign policy appear, particularly the open-door policy in the aftermath of Tiananmen. But those disputes appear to have involved Deng and other "retired" leaders of the CCP more than they actively involved younger formal leaders. Certainly, Li Peng, who sided with more conservative older critics of the open door, did not suffer for disagreeing with Deng on this issue (and others).[13]

It is always difficult to disentangle the policy and power elements of elite contestation in China. After political power has been reallocated, especially in the cases of informal processes associated with power struggles, purges, and involuntary removals from office, limited foreign policy criticisms of the losers in these struggles appear. Foreign policy actions have been and can be used as clubs in elite conflict. But overwhelmingly, foreign policy has never been the focal issue that causes top leaders to lose confidence in their putative successors, nor has it been the issue over which designated successors have gone to the mat to establish independent political bases. It is not clear whether this pattern will hold indefinitely into the future, however, given China's much greater involvement in the international system after more than two decades of the open-door policy.

It is relatively easy to explain why foreign policy has not been a critical component of struggles for power. First, foreign policy has tended to be dominated by the top leader, with Mao and Deng effectively controlling this issue area for about forty years of the PRC's fifty-four years of existence. Second, the vertical nature of decision making and the creation of policy systems (*xitong*) have kept the number of players and involved parties in foreign policymaking probably smaller than most other issues arenas. More importantly, it has kept many potentially involved parties, such as subnational units (provinces), out of foreign policymaking, at least formally. Finally, from the above factors, foreign policy involvement has not been a springboard for further political advance. Foreign ministry leaders have careers in the ministry. The minister or retired minister may become a vice premier, whose expertise is valued, but such a career has not been the basis for higher political advance. With efforts to professionalize the military, and the growing separation of military and political elites, military leaders have limited potential to use foreign policy to advance their political careers. This is not to say that the stakes of Chinese foreign policymaking are limited. They are confined, and short of absolute disasters, have tended to have limited political consequences.[14]

Institutions and Foreign Policy under the
Fourth Generation of Leaders

While the politics of elite succession will undoubtedly color Chinese foreign-policy decision making, the growing institutionalization of the Chinese polity will also influence outcomes as well. Certainly, there are institutions with clear missions involving China's position in the world. These would include the PLA and the Ministry of Foreign Affairs. But arguably, nearly every institution and interest in China has some sort of stake in China's open-door policy. Even apparently disadvantaged or highly protected sectors, such as workers in state-owned enterprises, grain-growing peasants, key industrial sectors in the information industry, and interior provinces can and do see some benefits from the open door in terms of capital, technology, policy advice, and propaganda. For the most part, even the apparent losers in the policy process accept the open-door policy (particularly after WTO accession). They can hinder implementation, demand internal or external compensation for market adjustments and the like, but so far, most interests in China have concluded that there is no alternative to the open door, and for many, the door needs to be further opened (at least in terms of flows of capital and technology), not closed or restricted, to deal with disadvantaged sectors.

The point of this is twofold. Under one scenario, with succession arrangements thrown into question, institutions and interests in the Chinese political system will continue to pay avid attention to China's role in the world, and to Chinese foreign policy broadly defined. With the leadership divided and focused on a struggle for power, they will seek opportunities to take maximum (and probably short-term) advantage of policy "flexibility"; try to evade constraints, as posed by the WTO; and otherwise try to do what they want while the leadership is focused on the elite power struggle.

Under the second scenario, assuming that Jiang gives up a quest for prolonged power without much more additional damage to political institutionalization, the fourth generation of leaders will gradually inherit leadership over the existing bodies of foreign policymaking, the most important of which are the FALSG, CMC, and Taiwan Affairs Leadership Small Group.[15] However, even if Hu Jintao were to obtain all of Jiang's three top posts smoothly, it is not clear that he would necessarily take over the leadership of China's foreign policy apparatus. After Jiang replaced Zhao Ziyang as general secretary, and replaced Deng Xiaoping as CMC chairman in 1989, Deng continued to exercise leadership over China's foreign relations, at least until 1992. At the time, Jiang had limited experience in foreign affairs, and with China's international position profoundly weakened by Tiananmen, there were limited opportunities for him to travel abroad and acquire both experience and international stature. Moreover, the post-Tiananmen period, ending with the collapse of the Soviet Union in late 1991, was a particularly complex and difficult one for Chinese foreign policymakers. The leadership was split on what to do about policies toward the West, the disintegrating socialist community, and the Soviet Union. Jiang undoubtedly could not manage such relations unchallenged. Either Deng held on to leadership here, or Jiang deferred to him. In any event, General Secretary Jiang did not control the foreign policymaking apparatus upon his ascension to the top post in 1989.

In addition, it was only in 1997 that General Secretary Jiang became the leader of the FALSG. Throughout much of the history of the FALSG, the premier has been its leader. In the 1950s and into the 1960s, Zhou Enlai headed it. Like many organizations, it seems to have been inactive during the Cultural Revolution decade, but when the FALSG was revived in 1977 (and until 1987), it was headed by Li Xiannian, a top political figure who was the president of the PRC in the mid-1980s. From 1987 to 1997, Premier Li Peng headed it.[16] And despite Li Peng's and Jiang Zemin's leading organizational role in the foreign policymaking apparatus, much of the key foreign policy advice and day-to-day guidance of foreign relations from the late 1980s to the present appears to come from former foreign minister Qian Qichen.

Like Jiang in 1989, Hu Jintao's foreign affairs experience is limited, although over the last several years, particularly in his capacity as vice president of the PRC, he has traveled fairly extensively, and has had meetings with major foreign leaders because he was regarded as Jiang's successor. But his foreign policy viewpoints and inclinations remain hard to discern. In short, even if the succession goes smoothly, it is unclear that Hu Jintao will automatically inherit real leadership over the top foreign-policy coordinating body in China, nor is it clear that he is capable of seizing control over the foreign policy agenda. As with recent U.S. presidents who have backgrounds as state governors, Hu and his colleagues in the fourth generation will rely heavily on foreign policy experts, probably of their generation.

Among those who will be involved in the foreign policymaking process are Vice Premier Wu Yi, a member of the Politburo, who was deeply involved with China's negotiations on WTO accession and foreign economic issues more generally, as well as State Councilor Tang Jiaxuan,

Foreign Minister Li Zhaoxing, Vice Foreign Minister Dai Bingguo, and Central Affairs Office Director Liu Huaqiu (all four of whom were elected to the Central Committee).[17] Qian Qichen may take over the "informal" position as manager of the Taiwan relationship, perhaps replacing the elderly Wang Daohan as the head of the Association for Relations Across the Taiwan Strait. Again, the outcome remains unclear about the powers of these individuals. Wu Yi was promoted and, given her experience, will likely retain management of foreign economic activity. Tang Jiaxuan has not had a distinguished career as foreign minister. Liu Huaqiu has had ups and downs in his career, and seems to have lost some influence in recent years. Li Zhaoxing and Dai Bingguo have become the key staffers in the post–16th Party Congress foreign-policy apparatus.

In trying to predict the future courses of Chinese foreign policy and their connections to domestic political issues, particularly generational and political succession, two basic alternatives need to be considered. In the first, Jiang goes to the mat either to retain his own power, or to promote his clients to the top spots in the formal leadership. This may not mean that he wins in this effort, but it does mean that a number of formal and informal norms and procedures will be violated. He will have violated the informal norm on retirement and arrangements set in place as early as 1992 to stage an orderly succession. Even if Jiang does retire, heavy-handed efforts to work through his clients in the fourth generation may violate norms and expectations about what older, retired leaders are supposed to do. Once these norms and procedures are violated, they will be very hard to reestablish. This does not foreshadow Stalinist-style purges among the leadership, but it does suggest substantial uncertainty among the elite, with some consequences for political action and foreign policy to be discussed below.

The other basic alternative is that the succession scenario unfolds largely as it seemed to be planned, with only a minimum of last-minute political jockeying taking place. Even if the succession goes smoothly, there remain substantial uncertainties about the foreign policymaking apparatus, and who is ultimately in charge.

However, within about five years, the fourth generation of leaders is likely to be dominating the political leadership, both formally and informally. Despite ambiguity about who will control the foreign policymaking apparatus at both the day-to-day and ultimate levels, one should expect Hu Jintao to play an active role in China's international relations. As *the* head of state and, eventually, chairman of the CMC, he will be seen by international society as the person who speaks for China, even as China's personification in international affairs. Hu will also be (presumably) the person with the ultimate power of decision on China's nuclear weapons use. These two characteristics give Hu unique power resources that inhere in his titular positions. He could use the former source of authority frequently with foreign visits and receiving foreign heads of state. He does not have to say anything for others to recognize the power that his command and control of China's nuclear weapons gives him. As Franz Schurmann pointed out thirty years ago, foreign affairs and nuclear weapons greatly expand the power of executives.[18] To strengthen his position, Hu will have an interest in being an activist in foreign affairs, even if there is little policy change. More generally, Hu's position is strengthened by a peaceful international environment, relative quiescence on the Taiwan issue, and continued rapid growth at home, with the foreign sector playing a significant role.

While Hu is gaining publicity and photo opportunities, management of foreign affairs will probably be highly bureaucratized. At one level, this means that professional foreign-affairs specialists, especially in the foreign ministry, military, and foreign trade bureaucracy, will staff key positions, write position papers, and formulate options. This suggests a fairly well-institutionalized foreign policymaking system. But at another level, it also suggests growing bureaucratic politics influencing foreign policymaking. As is the case in many other major powers, there is a suspicion among conservatives and some military figures that foreign ministry personnel emphasize diplomacy—and would do anything to avoid major conflict. In short, foreign ministry officials are seen as too cosmopolitan or insufficiently attentive to national interests. Often, military institutions are seen (in a reverse image) as the embodiment of robust nationalisms that at the least may lead to inadvertent spirals of threat and reaction. Foreign trade officials emphasize business. These stereotypes are overly broad, but views like those sketched above have been making the rounds of the Beijing rumor mills for years.

The military can be expected to see the Taiwan issue and Sino-American relations as the most important foreign policy questions for China, and to weigh in extensively with PLA perspectives on those issues. Sino-Russian, Sino-Japanese, and Sino-Indian relations will be of secondary importance. While not tolerant of movement toward Taiwan independence, the PLA's position on many of these issues is not set in stone. It continually evaluates U.S. military strength. At the same time, it is also concerned about Japanese discussions of nuclear weapons development and an expanded or more "normal" role for Japan in international affairs. A wary eye is kept on a developing India. The PLA continues to see Russia as its major source of advanced military technology. But these perspectives do not translate into absolute policy positions (with the possible exception of Taiwan), and actual PLA advocacy on foreign policy and security issues will probably depend on specific developments, incidents, and unanticipated events. Regardless of specific foreign policy circumstances, the PLA will continue to advocate the need for military modernization, and its prerequisite—an economic system that is capable of obtaining or producing the weapons that are needed to increase China's international capabilities.

Foreign ministry officials will likely continue to be the key staffers in the foreign policymaking apparatus. They probably do not disagree with military figures on the ultimate goals of China's foreign policy—to become a great power—but there may be significant differences about the means to those ends. Moreover, the two organizations may in fact have different definitions of what constitutes a great power; both would agree that military, economic, and scientific and technical modernization would be core components of China as a great power. Other things being equal, we might assume that foreign ministry officials will see more dimensions to Chinese foreign policy than will military officials, and may be open to a wider range of options in influencing international outcomes.

Foreign trade officials have a significant stake in the open-door policy, but this has ambiguous consequences for them and their organization. They mediate China's membership in the WTO, but WTO membership constrains the foreign trade bureaucracy's discretion. Foreign trade officials have historically had little influence in the domestic political economy, and certainly have had difficulty getting powerful domestic interests to follow foreign trade directives. WTO membership will require China to expand foreign trade rights to entities based in China, which will come at the expense of the profits of China's state-owned foreign trade corporations. Other than to say that foreign trade officials will emphasize foreign trade and investment, it is difficult to foresee more specific policy advocacy from this sector.

Thus, with the succession to the fourth generation working as intended, significant policy change in the relatively near term is not expected, other things being equal. The new leaders for the most part will not have great experience in foreign affairs. They will rely on their advisors and bureaucratic staffers to come up with options and policies, and they will debate the merits of various options. For the most part, Chinese foreign policy has been relatively successful in recent years, and one would not expect to see major changes in it, again, other things being equal. Bureaucratic conflict over foreign policy is likely to increase, at least until the new leadership has obtained a certain amount of confidence in its ability to master Chinese foreign policy. Before then, various bureaucracies will be competing to see which will be the most influential on the leadership for policy advice and recommendations. From a purely political point of view, the PLA brings much more to the table in this bureaucratic process than do most, if not all, other bureaucracies. It may be able to deliver tangible political support in exchange for policy involvement in ways that the foreign ministry and other units cannot.

But in the post–September 11 world, other things are not equal. From China's perspective, there is great uncertainty in the international environment, particularly concerning the way the United States defines itself as a world actor and the actual actions it takes. Coupled with a Japan that seems more inclined to develop its military forces in the coming years, China's perception of the international environment may become more negative, and a sense of threat to China would grow. International economic shocks may also severely shake the assumptions guiding China's overall international orientation. Given Japan's proximity, and the unilateral military superiority of the United States, diplomatic "solutions" to a perceived deteriorating security environment will not go very far. China will continue to push for growing economic interdependence with Japan and the United States as perhaps a way to temper potential security conflicts, but realists in all three nations will try to temper this approach as well, particularly if interdependence means China running substantial trade surpluses. Ultimately, China would likely accelerate its already steady military modernization. Since China's existing military modernization is seen by the Pentagon and others as a threat to U.S. security, an arms race between the United States and China is likely to ensue.

If instead of orderly succession, an expanding power struggle emerges in the near future, the rules of the game in Chinese politics will be extremely muddied, creating greatly heightened uncertainty within the elite, and the prospects for Chinese foreign policy will be considerably less clear. As noted, even if Jiang stays on, his victory is likely to be only temporary, as he ages. Around him, his clients will likely compete with each other to be his ultimate successor. Whether Jiang will have the power and authority to make his decisions stick with his followers is anyone's guess.

Perhaps increased contestation for power will emerge among Zeng Qing-hong, Wu Bangguo, and Huang Ju, making Jiang's attempt to use them as a group moot.

Certainly, attempts by Jiang (or others) to violate the existing succession arrangements will anger, upset, and mobilize many against him and his followers. How this would play itself out is impossible to determine. But the overall consequence of Jiang's moves would be to even more deeply politicize all issues in China, including foreign policy. Foreign policy would likely remain a subsidiary issue, but one that various groups could use for point scoring and trying to build and sustain various coalitions within the Chinese political spectrum. This politicization of all issues would spread to the bureaucracies, as bureaucratic professionalism would not be seen as a virtue in the context of ongoing power struggle where the rules of the game are at best ambiguous. This means that the key bureaucracies would be factionalized.

Again, assuming that there are not major changes in the world over the next five years or so, intense elite conflict over power in China may not severely damage all Chinese foreign policy. Policy inertia may be a relatively safe option for many. But whether foreign investors would continue to invest, whether Taiwan's leaders would try to expand the envelope of Taiwan's international status, and so on, are far from clear. China's potential leadership disarray will appear to make China look weak, and this is either an invitation for others to try to take advantage of China, or a sign that one cannot rely on the future to look like the recent past. Political conflict will be bad for China's international orientation and status. The injection of "hot-button" issues like Taiwan independence or low growth rates due to declining foreign investment and trade will exacerbate leadership conflict. Under such pressure and politicization, the Chinese foreign policy process is likely to deviate very substantially from a model of rational decision making.

Jiang Zemin's seeming unwillingness to abide by succession arrangements risks untold damage for China's international position and, indeed, for China's future. Even if the succession works out as planned, China faces a complicated, contradictory, and novel international environment, which will be hard to understand and adapt to in the best of circumstances. It is by no means clear that the fourth generation is up to the job, but if the power struggle over succession worsens, it is all but guaranteed that China will adopt dysfunctional foreign policies.

Notes

1. Andrew J. Nathan and Bruce Gilley, *China's New Rulers: The Secret Files* (N.Y.: New York Review of Books, 2002). The results of the leadership decisions at the 16th Party Congress and subsequent meeting of the first plenary session of the 16th Central Committee are widely available. For one source, see www.china.org.cn/english/features/45340.htm.

2. The importance and decisiveness of different levels of analysis (system, nation, bureaucratic, and individual) are well discussed in nearly canonical fashion by Robert Jervis in his *Perception and Misperception in International Politics* (Princeton, N.J.: Princeton University Press, 1976), chapter 1.

3. For suggestive insights on the thinking of the fourth generation of leaders, see Nathan and Gilley, *China's New Rulers*, note 1, and Cheng Li, *China's Leaders: The New Generation* (Lanham, Md.: Rowman & Littlefield, 2001).

4. The best known of these is Kenneth N. Waltz, *Theory of International Politics* (Menlo Park, Calif.: Addison Wesley, 1977).

5. D. Ravi Kanth, "China: New and 'Pushy' Boy on the Block," *Asia Times,* February 7, 2002.

6. James Kynge, "China's Reverse Shock," *Financial Times*, June 7, 2002.

7. Jeffrey E. Garten, "When Everything Is Made in China," *Business Week*, June 17, 2002, and Barry Lynn, "Unmade in America," *Harper's Magazine*, June 2002.

8. Erik Eckholm, "China's President May Be Reluctant to Cede His Power," *New York Times*, July 13, 2002; Susan V. Lawrence and Charles Hutzler, "China's Jiang Is Likely to Retain Top Spots, Impeding Power Shift," *Wall Street Journal*, September 4, 2002; and John Pomfret, "Chinese Leader Throws a Curve," *Washington Post*, July 21, 2002.

9. Nathan and Gilley, *China's New Rulers*, 65–73.

10. "Jiang Hopes to Leave Legacy Whether He Goes or Stays," Reuters, September 12, 2002.

11. For an early overview on the connections between domestic politics and Chinese foreign policy, see Harry Harding, "Linkages Between Chinese Domestic Politics and Foreign Policy" (paper presented at Workshop on Chinese Foreign Policy, Ann Arbor, Mich., August 12–14, 1976).

12. The new scholarship on Lin, doubting earlier views of foreign policy differences, includes Frederick C. Teiwes and Warren Sun, *The Tragedy of Lin Biao* (Honolulu: University of Hawaii Press, 1996), and Jin Qiu, *The Culture of Power* (Stanford, Calif.: Stanford University Press, 1999). On the foreign trade issue, see Ann Fenwick, "Chinese Foreign Trade Policy and the Campaign Against Deng Xiaoping," in *China's Quest for Independence*, ed. Thomas Fingar (Boulder, Colo.: Westview Press, 1980), 199–224.

13. Joseph Fewsmith, *China Since Tiananmen* (Cambridge: Cambridge University Press, 2001), chapter 1.

14. On these points, see David Bachman, "Structure and Process in the Making of Chinese Foreign Policy," in *China and the World*, 4th ed., ed. Samuel S. Kim (Boulder, Colo: Westview Press, 1998), 34–54.

15. There is a substantial body of fine scholarship on Chinese foreign policy decision-making practices and institutions. See Lu Ning, *The Dynamics of Foreign Policy Decision Making in China*, 2d ed. (Boulder, Colo.: Westview Press, 2000); Michael D.

Swaine, *The Role of the Chinese Military in National Security Policy Making* (Santa Monica, Calif.: Rand Corporation, 1996); and David M. Lampton, ed., *The Making of Chinese Foreign and Security Policy in the Era of Reform* (Stanford, Calif.: Stanford University Press, 2001).

16. Lu, *The Dynamics of Foreign Policy Decision Making in China*, 10–11.

17. Benjamin Kang Lim, "Top Contenders Emerge to Oversee Chinese Foreign Policy," Reuters, November 6, 2002.

18. Franz Schurmann, *The Logic of World Power* (N.Y.: Pantheon Books, 1974), especially part 1.

Chronology

1989

May	Jiang Zemin internally designated as Party general secretary
June 4	Tiananmen crackdown
June 23–24	Fourth Plenary Session of the Thirteenth Central Committee; Jiang's appointment as general secretary confirmed at the meeting
November 6–9	Fifth Plenary Session of the Thirteenth Central Committee; Deng Xiaoping transfers his Party Central Military Commission chairmanship to Jiang Zemin

1990

March 9–12	Sixth Plenary Session of the Thirteenth Central Committee; Party-mass relationships emphasized

1991

March	Zhu Rongji promoted as vice-premier
July 1	Jiang Zemin called for opposing "peaceful evolution" to capitalism

1992

January–February	Deng Xiaoping takes "southern tour" to promote economic reform
October 12–19	Fourteenth Party Congress convenes; Hu Jintao promoted to the Politburo Standing Committee, Wu Bangguo and Wen Jiabao to the Politburo

1993

March   Eighth National People Congress; Jiang assumes
                          PRC presidency
September   Beijing loses bid for hosting 2000 Olympics

1994

September 25–28   Fourth Plenary Session of the Fourteenth Central
                          Committee; transfer of the supreme power from
                          Deng to Jiang completed

1995

January 31   Jiang announces his "eight points" regarding rela-
                          tions with Taiwan
April   Chen Yun dies; Beijing Party Secretary Chen Xitong
                          purged for corruption
June   Taiwanese leader Lee Teng-hui visits the United
                          States

1996

March   Taiwan holds first popular presidential election

1997

February 19   Deng Xiaoping dies
July 1   Hong Kong is returned to China
September 12–18   Fifteenth Party Congress convenes; Qiao Shi retires
                          from the Politburo Standing Committee
October 28   Jiang Zemin visits the United States

1998

March   Ninth National People's Congress convenes; Zhu
                          Rongji takes premiership and announces major
                          government restructuring
June   President Clinton visits China
July   China Democratic Party announces its birth

1999

April 25	Falun Gong demonstration around Zhongnanhai compound
May	Hu Jintao makes a TV speech after bombing of Chinese embassy in Belgrade
September 19–22	Hu Jintao promoted to vice chairman of Party Central Military Commission
November 12	United States and China reach agreement on China's entry into WTO

2000

February	Jiang Zemin announces "Three Representations" as a new Party goal

2001

April 1	Chinese fighter collides with U.S. E-P3 surveillance plane
July 1	Jiang Zemin makes a speech at the 80th anniversary of the founding of the Chinese Communist Party
July 13	China selected to host 2008 Olympics Games
December 11	China joins WTO

2002

May 31	Jiang Zemin makes a speech at the Central Party School
November 8–15	Sixteenth Party Congress convenes. Hu Jintao succeeds Jiang as Party general secretary. Jiang retains CMC chairmanship

Selected Bibliography

Bachman, David. "Structure and Process in the Making of Chinese Foreign Policy." In *China and the World*, 4th ed., ed. Samuel S. Kim, 34–54. Boulder, Colo.: Westview Press, 1998.

———. "Succession, Consolidation, and Transition in China's Future." *Journal of Northeast Asian Studies* 15 (1996): 89–106.

———. *Bureaucracy, Economy, and Leadership in China: The Institutional Origins of the Great Leap Forward*. Cambridge: Cambridge University Press, 1991.

Bates, Robert H., ed. *Toward a Political Economy of Development*. Berkeley: University of California Press, 1988.

Baum, Richard. "To Reform or to Muddle Through? The Challenges Facing China's Fourth Generation." In *Asia Program Special Report: The 16th CCP Congress and Leadership Transition in China*. Washington, D.C.: Woodrow Wilson International Center for Scholars, 2002.

Becker, Jasper. *The Chinese*. N.Y.: Free Press, 2000.

Boycko, Maxim, Andrei Shleifer, and Robert Vishny. *Privatizing Russia*. Cambridge, Mass.: MIT Press, 1997.

Brinton, Mary C., and Victor Nee, eds. *The New Institutionalism in Sociology*. Cambridge: Cambridge University Press, 2001.

Byrd, William. *Chinese Industrial Firms under Reform*. Washington, D.C.: World Bank, 1992.

———. *The Market Mechanism and Economic Reform in China*. Armonk, N.Y.: M.E. Sharpe, 1991.

Cao, Jinqing. *China along the Yellow River: A Scholar's Observations and Meditations on Chinese Rural Society*. Shanghai: Wenyi Chubanshe, 2000.

Chai, Joseph C.H. *China: Transition to a Market Economy*. N.Y.: Oxford University Press, 1997.

Chan, Anita. *China's Workers under Assault: The Exploitation of Labor in a Globalizing Economy*. Armonk, N.Y.: M.E. Sharpe, 2001.

China's State Statistics Bureau. *Statistical Yearbook of China*. Beijing: China Statistical Publishing House, various years.

Chou, Oliver. "Rising Up the PLA Ranks." *South China Morning Post,* April 25, 2002.

Crawford, Beverly, ed. *Markets, States, and Democracy: The Political Economy of Post-Communist Transformation*. Boulder, Colo.: Westview Press, 1995.

Crawford, Franklin. "Cornell ILR Researcher: Trade with China Hurts U.S. Labor Market." *Cornell Chronicle*, August 30, 2001.

Dahl, Robert. *Democracy and Its Critics.* New Haven, Conn.: Yale University Press, 1989.

Davis, Deborah S., ed. *The Consumer Revolution in Urban China.* Berkeley: University of California Press, 2000.

Demsetz, Harold, ed. *Ownership, Control, and the Firm: The Organization of Economic Activity.* Oxford: Blackwell, 1967.

Deng, Xiaoping. *Selected Works of Deng Xiaoping: 1975–1982.* Beijing: People's Press, 1983.

———. *Selected Works of Deng Xiaoping*, vol. 2. Beijing: People's Press, 1993.

Ding, Xueliang. "Systemic Irregularity and Spontaneous Property Transformation in the Chinese Financial Sector." *The China Quarterly* 163, no. 1 (2000): 655–676.

———."The Informal Asset Stripping of Chinese State Firms." *The China Journal* 43 (2000): 1–28.

———."Informal Privatization through Internationalization." *British Journal of Political Science* 30, no. 1 (2000).

———. "The Quasi-Criminalization of a Business Sector in China: Deconstructing the Construction Sector Syndrome." *Crime, Law, and Social Change* 35, no. 3 (2001): 177–201.

Dittmer, Lowell. *China under Reform.* Boulder, Colo.: Westview Press, 1994.

Dittmer, Lowell, Haruhiro Fukui, and Peter N.S. Lee, eds. *Informal Politics in East Asia.* Berkeley: University of California Press, 2000.

Dong, Yuyu, and Shi Binhai, eds. *Zhengzhi Zhongguo* [Chinese Politics]. Beijing: Jinri Zhongguo Chubanshe, 1998.

Eckholm, Erik. "Time for the Changing of China's Aging Guard—or Not." *The New York Times*, September 22, 2002.

Eggertsson, Thráinn. *Economic Behavior and Institutions.* Cambridge: Cambridge University Press, 1990.

Ellings, Richard J., and Aaron L. Friedberg, eds. *Strategic Asia: Power and Purpose, 2001–02.* Seattle: The National Bureau of Asian Research, 2001.

Elster, Jon. *The Cement of Society: A Study of Social Order.* Cambridge: Cambridge University Press, 1989.

Fewsmith, Joseph. *China since Tiananmen.* Cambridge: Cambridge University Press, 2001.

Fingar, Thomas, ed., *China's Quest for Independence.* Boulder, Colo.: Westview Press, 1980.

"Flight of Four Thousand Corrupt Officials" [in Chinese]. *Industrial and Commercial Times*, August 24, 2002.

"Flight of Mainland Capital over $50 Million in Three Years." *China Times*, September 11, 2002.

Gang, Xiong. "Lun Woguo Zhengzhi Tizhi Gaige de Lishi Yanjin he Zouxiang" [On the Development and Future Trend of China's Political Reform]. *Zhongguo Zhengzhi*, no. 1 (2002): 18.

Gao, Yaojie. "My AIDS Prevention Journey," trans. David Cowhig. Chinese original available at www.aizhi.org/jkwz/journey/htm.

Garten, Jeffrey E. "When Everything Is Made in China." *Business Week*, June 17, 2002.

Gregory, Neil, Stoyan Tenev, and Dileep Wagle. *China's Emerging Private Enterprises: Prospects for the New Century*. Washington, D.C.: International Finance Corporation, 2000.

Grossman, Sanford J., and Oliver D. Hart. "The Costs and Benefits of Ownership: A Theory of Vertical and Lateral Integration." *Journal of Political Economy* 94 (1986).

Haggard, Stephan. *Pathways from the Periphery: The Politics of Growth in the Newly Industrializing Countries*. Ithaca: Cornell University Press, 1990.

Harding, Harry. "Linkages between Chinese Domestic Politics and Foreign Policy" (paper presented at Workshop on Chinese Foreign Policy, Ann Arbor, Mich., August 12–14, 1976).

He, Ping, and Liu Siyang. "Dang de Xinyijie Zhongyang Weiyuanhui Danshengji" [The Birth of the New Central Committee of the CCP], available at www.xinhuanet.com, accessed on November 14, 2002.

He, Qinglian. "Comprehensive Analysis of Current Social Structural Changes in China." *Shuwu* 3 (2000).

———. *Xiandaihua de Xianjiang* [Pitfalls of Modernization]. Beijing: Jinri Zhongguo Chubanshe, 1998.

Hu, Angang. *China: Fighting against Corruption* [in Chinese]. Hangzhou: Zhejiang People's Publishing House, 2001.

Hu, Xiaobo. *Problems in China's Transitional Economy: Property Rights and Transitional Models*. Singapore: Singapore University Press, 1998.

———."Transformation of Property Rights in China: The Institutional Origins," Entrepreneurial Leadership Working Paper Series #02-101. Clemson, S.C.: The Arthur Spiro Center for Entrepreneurial Leadership, Clemson University, 2002.

Hu, Xiaobo, and Gang Lin, eds. *Transition towards Post-Deng China*. Singapore: Singapore University Press, 1998.

Hu, Wei. *Zhengfu Guocheng* [Process of Government]. Zhejiang: Zhejiang Renmin Chubanshe, 1998.

Huang, Yasheng. "Why China Will Not Collapse." *Foreign Policy* 99 (1995): 54–68.

Human Rights Watch. *Dangerous Meditation: China's Campaign Against Falun Gong*. N.Y.: Human Rights Watch, 2002.

Jennings, M. Kent. "Political Participation in the Chinese Countryside." *American Political Science Review* 91: 2 (1997).

Jervis, Robert. *Perception and Misperception in International Politics*. Princeton, N.J.: Princeton University Press, 1976.

Jiang, Changyun. "Rural Land and Social Security for Farmers." *Da Gong Bao* (Hong Kong), March 9, 2002 (Foreign Broadcast Information Service translation, March 15, 2002).

Jiang, Zemin. *Report to the 16th National Party Congress,* Beijing: Renmin Chubanshe, 2002.

———. "Speech at the 80th Anniversary of the Founding of the CCP." *People's Daily,* July 1, 2001.

Jin, Taijun. "Xinshiji Zhongguo Zhengzhi Gaige Ruogan Zhongda Wenti de Sikao." *Zhongguo Zhengzhi* [Chinese Politics] 11 (2001).

Johnson, Chalmers. *MITI and the Japanese Miracle: The Growth of Industrial Policy, 1925–1975.* Stanford, Calif.: Stanford University Press, 1982.

Kanth, D. Ravi. "China: New and 'Pushy' Boy on the Block." *Asia Times,* February 7, 2002.

Kynge, James. "China's Reverse Shock." *Financial Times,* June 7, 2002.

Kornai, János. *The Road to a Free Economy: Shifting from a Socialist System: The Example of Hungary.* N.Y.: W. W. Norton, 1990.

Lam, Willy Wo-Lap. "China's 'Dangerous' Class Divide Set to Stay," Cable Network News, September 3, 2002.

———."Rural Discontent Mounts," *South China Morning Post,* February 9, 2000, 13.

Lampton, David M., ed. *The Making of Chinese Foreign and Security Policy in the Era of Reform.* Stanford, Calif.: Stanford University Press, 2001.

Lau, Lawrence, Yingyi Qian, and Gerard Roland. "Reform without Losers: An Interpretation of China's Dual-Track Approach to Transition," Discussion Paper 1798. London: Center for Economic Policy Research, 1997.

Lawrence, Susan. "Three Cheers for the Party." *Far Eastern Economic Review,* October 26, 2000.

———."The New Leadership: It Ain't Over, Till It's Over." *Far Eastern Economic Review,* August 8, 2002, 24–25.

———.and Charles Hutzler, "China's Jiang Is Likely to Retain Top Spots, Impeding Power Shift." *Wall Street Journal,* September 4, 2002.

Lee, Peter N.S. *Industrial Management and Economic Reform in China, 1949–1984.* Hong Kong: Oxford University Press, 1987.

Li, Changping. *Wo Xiang Zongli Shuo Shihua* [Tell Truth to the Premier]. Beijing-Guangming Ribao Chubanshe, 2001.

Li, Cheng. *China's Leaders: The New Generation.* Lanham, Md.: Rowman & Littlefield, 2001.

Li, David D. "A Theory of Ambiguous Property Rights in Transition Economies: The Case of the Chinese Non-State Sector." *Journal of Comparative Economics* 23 (1996): 1–19.

Li, Huairen. "Jianshe Shehuizhuyi Zhengzhi Wenming de Silu yu Tupokou," [Some Thoughts on the Starting Point for Developing Socialist Political Civilization]. *Tizhi Gaige* [System Reform] no. 7 (2002).

Li, Junru. "Zhonggong Fen Sanjieduan Zhunbei Shiliuda Lilun" [The CCP Has Prepared the Theory for the 16th National Congress through Three Stages]. *Outlook* (Beijing), August 12, 2002.

Li, Lianjiang. "The Two-Ballot System in Shanxi Province: Subjecting Village Party Secretaries to a Public Vote." *The China Quarterly* 42 (1999).

Li, Yongzhong. "Guanyu Gaige Dangwei 'Yixing Heyi' Lingdao Tizhi de Sikao" [On Reforming the Ruling System of "Combining Executive and Legislative Functions into One Organ" within Party Committees]. *Tizhi Gaige,* no. 4 (2002).

Li, Zhongjie. "Yi Gaige de Jingsheng Ba Dang de Jianshe Tuixiang Qianjin" [Promoting Party-Building with the Reform Spirit], available at www.xinhuanet.com, accessed on September 11, 2002.

Liang, Si. "China Makes Earnest Preparations for 16th Party Congress to Be Held in Second Half of this Year." *Zhongguo Tongxun She* (Hong Kong), January 7, 2002.

Lim, Benjamin Kang. "Top Contenders Emerge to Oversee Chinese Foreign Policy." Reuters, November 6, 2002.

Lin, Gang. "China's Democratic Prospect in the Post-Deng Era." In *Transition towards Post-Deng China*, ed. Xiaobo Hu and Gang Lin. Singapore: Singapore University Press, 2001, 253–255.

Lin, Gang, and Weixing Chen, *Prospects for Cross-Taiwan Strait Development*. Hong Kong: Asian Science Press, 2000.

Lin, Kun-Chin. "Markets and Hierarchies in Post-Socialism: Theory and Evidence from the Chinese Oil Industry," paper presented at Annual Meeting of the American Political Science Association, San Francisco, Calif., September 1, 2001.

Link, Perry, Richard Madsen, and Paul Pickowicz, eds. *Popular China: Unofficial Culture in a Globalizing Society*. Lanham, Md.: Rowman & Littlefield, 2002.

Liu Junning. "The Intellectual Turn: The Emergence of Liberalism in Contemporary China." In *China's Future: Constructive Partner or Emerging Threat?* ed. Ted Galen Carpenter and James A. Dorn. Washington, D.C.: Cato Institute, 2000.

Liu, Shibai. "Merger as an Important Form in Transforming Property Rights of the Enterprises" [in Chinese]. *People's Daily*, February 3, 1989, 5h.

Liu, Yantang. "Party Building over 13 Years—Interviewing with Lu Xianfu," *Xinhuanet*, September 24, 2002, available at www.xinhuanet.com, accessed on September 24, 2002.

Lo, Ping. "Jiang Zemin Verbally Confers Title of 'Principal Core' [zhuti hexin] on Hu, Zeng." *Cheng Ming*, October 1, 2001, 12–13.

Lu, Hanlong. "To Be Relatively Comfortable in an Egalitarian Society." In *The Consumer Revolution in Urban China*, ed. Deborah S. Davis. Berkeley: University of California Press, 2000, 124–141.

Lu, Xueyi. "The Peasants Are Suffering, The Villages Are Very Poor." *Dushu*, January 2001. Trans. David Cowhig, available at www.usembassychina.org.cn/english/sandt/villages.html.

Lynn, Barry. "Unmade in America." *Harper's Magazine*, June 2002.

Ma, Licheng, and Ling Zhijun. *Jiaofeng* [Confrontation]. Beijing: Jinri Zhongguo Chubanshe, 1998.

McFaul, Michael. "The Allocation of Property Rights in Russia: The First Round." *Communist and Post-Communist Studies* 29, no. 3 (1996) 287–308.

MacGregor, James. *Leadership.* N.Y.: Harper & Row, 1978.

Madsen, Richard. *China's Catholics: Tragedy and Hope in an Emerging Civil Society.* Berkeley: University of California Press, 1998.

———. *Morality and Power in a Chinese Village.* Berkeley: University of California Press, 1984.

Manion, Melanie. *Retirement of Revolutionaries in China: Public Policies, Social Norms, Private Interests.* Princeton, N.J.: Princeton University Press, 1993.

Mao, Zedong. *Selected Works of Mao Zedong*, vol. 2. Beijing: Remin Chubanshe, 1986.

McElroy, Damien. "Jiang Stamps Authority with Five More Years at Top." *The Scotsman*, August 26, 2002, available at http://search.scotsman.com/scripts/rwisapi.dll/@network.env, accessed on August 29, 2002.

McKinnon, Ronald I. *The Order of Economic Liberalization: Financial Control in the Transition to a Market Economy.* Baltimore: The Johns Hopkins University Press, 1993.

Milor, Vedat. *Changing Political Economies: Privatization in Post-Communist and Reforming Communist States.* Boulder, Colo.: Lynne Rienner Publications, 1994).

Moore, Barrington. *Social Origins of Dictatorship and Democracy.* Boston: Beacon Press, 1966.

Murphy, Rachel. "Return Migration, Entrepreneurship and Local State Corporatism in Rural China: The Experience of Two Counties in South Jiangxi." *Journal of Contemporary China* 9, no. 24 (2000): 231–247.

Nathan, Andrew, and Bruce Gilley. "China's New Rulers: What They Want." *New York Review of Books*, October 10, 2002.

Nee, Victor. "Organizational Dynamics of Market Transition: Hybrid Forms, Property Rights, and Mixed Economy in China." *Administrative Science Quarterly* 37, no. 1 (1992): 1–27.

Ning, Lu. *The Dynamics of Foreign Policy Decision Making in China*, 2d ed. Boulder, Colo.: Westview Press, 2000.

North, Douglass C. *Institutions, Institutional Change, and Economic Performance.* Cambridge and N.Y.: Cambridge University Press, 1990.

O'Donnell, Lynn. "Armed Police to Break Standoff." *The Australian*, March 20, 2002.

Oi, Jean C., and Andrew G. Walder, eds. *Property Rights and Economic Reform in China.* Stanford, Calif.: Stanford University Press, 1999.

Olson, Mancur. *The Rise and Decline of Nations: Economic Growth, Stagflation, and Social Rigidities.* New Haven: Yale University Press, 1982.

"On Party Congresses—Remarks by Xie Chuntao." *Xinhuanet*, November 6, 2002, available at www.xinhuanet.com, accessed on November 6, 2002.

Page, Jeremy. "China Opens Up Political Debate to Strengthen Party." *Reuters News*, July 20, 2000.

Parish, William L., and Martin King Whyte. *Village and Family in Contemporary China.* Chicago: University of Chicago Press, 1978.

Pei, Minxin. *From Reform to Revolution: The Demise of Communism in China and the Soviet Union.* Cambridge, Mass.: Harvard University Press, 1994.

Peng, Kailei, and Ma Haiyan. "Turnover of Top Provincial and Municipal Officials to Greet 16th CPC Congress." *Wen Wei Po* (Hong Kong), March 2, 2002, A5.

Phillips, Michael, et al. "Suicide Rates in China, 1995–99." *Lancet* 359 (2002).

Pomfret, John. "Chinese Capitalists Gain New Legitimacy: Ties to State Pay Off for Some Ventures." *Washington Post*, September 29, 2002, A01.

Pomfret, John, and Philip P. Pan, "China's Leader Opens Party to the Country's New Rich." *Washington Post*, November 8, 2002, A21.

Poznanski, Kazimierz Z., ed. *The Evolutionary Transition to Capitalism.* Boulder, Colo.: Westview Press, 1995.

Przeworski, Adam. *Democracy and the Market: Political and Economic Reforms in Eastern Europe and Latin America.* Cambridge: Cambridge University Press, 1991.

Qin Hui. "Ershi Shiji Mo Zhongguo de Jingji Zhuangui, Shehui Gongzheng yu Minzhuhua Wenti" [Issues on China's Economic Transformation, Social Justice and Democratization at the end of the 20th Century]. In *Political Science and China in Transition.* Beijing: Renmin University of China, July 2002.

Qiu, Jin. *The Culture of Power.* Stanford, Calif.: Stanford University Press, 1999.

Readon, Lawrence C. "The Death Knell of China's Command Economy?—The WTO and China's State-Owned Enterprises." *China Enters the WTO: The Death Knell for State-Owned Enterprises,* ed. Gang Lin. *Asia Program Special Report* 103. Washington, D.C.: Woodrow Wilson International Center for Scholars, June 2002, 7–10.

Rosenthal, Elisabeth. "China's Communists Try to Decide What They Stand For." *New York Times,* May 1, 2002.

Schurmman, Franz. *The Logic of World Power.* N.Y.: Pantheon Books, 1974.

Shi, Tianjian, "Cultural Values and Democracy in the People's Republic of China." *China Quarterly* 162 (2000): 540–559.

Shirk, Susan L. *The Political Logic of Economic Reform in China.* Berkeley: University of California Press, 1993.

Schroeder, Gertrude E. "Property Rights Issues in Economic Reforms in Socialist Countries." *Studies in Comparative Communism* 21, no. 2 (1988): 175-88.

Solinger, Dorothy J. *From Lathes to Looms: China's Industrial Policy in Comparative Perspective, 1979-1982,* Stanford: Stanford University Press, 1991.

———. "WTO and China's Workers." *Asia Program Special Report* 103. Washington, D.C.: Woodrow Wilson International Center for Scholars, June 2002.

"Special Dispatch: Young Cadres Will Be Selected to Head Provinces and Ministries," *Ming Pao*, November 4, 2000.

Su, Shaozhi. "Critiquing the 'Three Represents' Theory." *Cheng Ming*, July 2000, 45–53.

Swaine, Michael D. *The Role of the Chinese Military in National Security Policy Making.* Santa Monica, Calif.: Rand Corporation, 1996.

Teiwes, Frederick C., and Warren Sun. *The Tragedy of Lin Biao.* Honolulu: University of Hawaii Press, 1996.

Teiwes, Frederick, and Jin Qiu, *The Culture of Power* (Stanford, Calif.: Stanford University Press, 1999).

Tian, Guoqiang. "Property Rights and the Nature of Chinese Collective Enterprises." *Journal of Comparative Economics* 28 (2000): 247–268.

Tien, Hung-mao, and Yun-han Chu, eds. *China under Jiang Zemin.* Boulder, Colo.: Lynne Rienner Publishers, 2000.

"TIME Magazine: Majority of Chinese Start-Ups Gain Wealth Illegally" [in Chinese], September 17, 2002, available at: www.zaobao.com/special/newspapers/2002/09/others170902d.html, accessed on September 17, 2002.

Tong, Christopher S.P. "Total Factor Productivity Growth and Its Spatial Disparity across China's Township and Village Enterprises." *Journal of Contemporary China* 10, no. 26 (2001): 155–171.

Unger, Jonathan. *The Nature of Chinese Politics: From Mao to Jiang.* Armonk, N.Y.: M.E. Sharpe, 2002.

Uvalic, Milica, and Daniel Vaughan-Whitehead. *Privatization Surprises in Transition Economies: Employee-Ownership in Central and Eastern Europe.* Cheltenham, UK: Edward Elgar Publishing Limited, 1997.

Vogel, Ezra F. *One Step Ahead in China: Guangdong under Reform.* Cambridge, Mass.: Harvard University Press, 1989.

Walder, Andrew G. *Communist Neo-Traditionalism: Work and Authority in Chinese Industry.* Berkeley: University of California Press, 1986.

Walder, Andrew G. "Corporate Organization and Local Government Property Rights in China." In *Changing Political Economies: Privatization in Post-Communist and Reforming Communist States*, ed. Vedat Milor. Boulder, Colo.: Lynne Rienner Publishers, 1994, 58–66.

——— "The State as an Ensemble of Economic Actors: Some Inferences from China's Trajectory of Change." In *Transforming Post-Communist Political Economies*, ed. Joan Nelson, Charles Tilly, and Lee Walker, 432–452. Washington, D.C.: National Academy Press, 1998.

Waltz, Kenneth N. *Theory of International Politics.* Menlo Park, Calif.: Addison Wesley, 1977.

Wan, Bing, and Xue Guangzhou. *Minzhu Zexue* [Philosophy of Democracy]. Zhejiang: Zhejiang Remin Chubanshe, 1994.

Wang, Bangzuo, and Xie Yue. "Zhengdang Tuidong: Zhongguo Zhengzhi Tizhi Gaige de Yanzhang Luoji" [Party's Initiative: Logic of Chinese Political Reform]. *Chinese Politics*, no. 8 (2001).

Wang, Changjiang et al. *Xinshiji Dang de Jianshe de Weida Gangling—Xuexi Jiang*

Zemin Zongshuji Qiyi Jianghua [Jiang Zemin's "July 1" Speech]. Beijing: Central Party School Press, 2001.

Wang, Fei-ling. "Floaters, Moonlighters, and the Underemployed: A National Labor Market with Chinese Characteristics." *Journal of Contemporary China* 7, no. 19 (1998): 459–475.

Wang, Jingsong. *Zhonghua Renmin Gongheguo de Zhengfu he Zhengzhi* [The Government and Politics of the People's Republic of China]. Beijing: Zhongyang Dangxiao Chubanshe, 1994).

Weng, Jieming et al., eds. *Yu Zongshuji Tanxin* [Talking with the General Secretary]. Beijing: Zhongguo Shehui Kexue Chubanshe, 1996.

Winiecki, Jan. "Why Economic Reforms Fail in the Soviet System: A Property Rights-Based Approach." *Economic Inquiry* 28 (1990): 195–221.

World Bank. "China Reform of State Run Enterprises." *China Report* 14924, August 1996.

Xia, Wensi "Jiang Zemin Intends to Let Zeng Qinghong Assume Military Power." *Kaifang* (Hong Kong), January 1, 2002, 11–13.

Xie, Fangyi, "Zhengdang Xiandaihua: Zhizhengdang Mianlin de Yige Zhongda er Jinpo de Lilun yu Shijian Keti." *Tizhi Gaige* [System Reform] 9 (2001):15. (Originally published in *Ziliao Tongxun* [Materials and Communication], July/August, 9–13, 2001).

Yan, Renkuan. "Beijing Zhengtan Disandai" [Beijing's Third-Generation Politicians]. *Tide Monthly* (Hong Kong), 52 (1991): 12.

Yang, Deshan. "Developing Socialist Political Civilization," available at www.xinhuanet.com, accessed on September 6, 2002.

Ye, Weishi. "Sange Daibiao Zhongyao Sixiang Xingcheng he Fazhang Mailuo" [The Formation and Development of the Important Thought of "Three Represents"]. *Liberation Daily*, July 2, 2002.

Zhang, Li. *Strangers in the City: Reconfiguration of Space, Power, and Social Networks within China's Floating Population.* Stanford, Calif.: Stanford University Press, 2001.

Zhang, Liang. *The Tiananmen Papers*, ed. Andrew J. Nathan and Perry Link, with an afterword by Orville Schell. N.Y.: Public Affairs, 2001.

Zhang, Zhiming, "Ruling for the People and Party Building," Strengthening China Forum. *People's Daily*, July 30, 2002.

Zhong, Dajun. "China's Error: Adverse Impacts of China's Common Land System and Household Registration System on its Land Resources." *Guangzhou Xin Jingji*, March 20, 2001; Foreign Broadcast Information Service translation.

Zhou, Kate Xiao. *How the Farmers Changed China: Power to the People*. Boulder, Colo.: Westview Press, 1996.

Zhou, Ruipeng, Li Huiling, and Sun Chuanwei. "Ownership System of State Enterprises Clearly Defined" [in Chinese]. *Lianhe Zaobao* 28, November 9, 2002.

Zhu, Guanglei. *Dandai Zhongguo Zhengfu Guocheng* [Process of Government in Contemporary China]. Tianjin: Tianjin Renmin Chubanshe, 1997.

Contributors

David Bachman is professor at the Henry M. Jackson School of International Studies and chair of the China Studies Program at the University of Washington. He is the author of *Bureaucracy, Leadership, and Economy in China* (1991) and *Chen Yun and the Chinese Political System* (1985); and co-editor of *Yan Jiaqi and China's Struggle for Democracy* (1991). He writes frequently on Chinese domestic politics and foreign policy. He is completing a book on defense industrialization in China.

Lowell Dittmer is professor of political science at the University of California-Berkeley and editor of *Asian Survey*. He has authored four books, co-authored two books, co-edited three books, and conducted many other studies of Chinese domestic and foreign policy. His most recent works are *Informal Politics in East Asia* (co-editor, 2000); *Liu Shaoqi and the Chinese Cultural Revolution* (revised edition, 1997); *Chinese Politics under Reform* (1993); *China's Quest for National Identity* (co-editor, 1993); *Sino–Soviet Normalization and Its International Implications* (1992); and *China's Continuous Revolution: The Post-Revolution Epoch, 1949–1981* (1986).

Xiaobo Hu is associate professor of political science at Clemson University in South Carolina. He has been conducting research on the political economy of transition in China, property rights, and small-town development. His publications include *Transition towards Post-Deng China* (co-editor, 2001); *Problems in China's Transitional Economy: Property Rights and Transitional Models* (1998); *Interpreting U.S.–China–Taiwan Relations: China in the Post–Cold War Era* (co-editor, 1998); and *Cross-Strait Relations toward the 21st Century* (co-editor, 1998).

Gang Lin is program associate in the Woodrow Wilson Center's Asia Program. He served as president of the Association of Chinese Political

Studies from 1998 to 1999. He has co-edited *Transition towards Post-Deng China* (2001) and *Prospects for Cross–Taiwan Strait Developments* (2000); co-authored *Taiwan's Political Transition* (1997); and contributed numerous articles and book chapters on Chinese politics and cross-Taiwan Strait relations.

Richard Madsen is professor of sociology and associate director of the Center for Democratization and Economic Development at the University of California–San Diego, specializing in the sociology of ideas/culture/religion, political sociology, and Chinese society. He has authored three books, co-authored three books, and co-edited five books, in addition to numerous articles and book chapters. His most recent works are *Meaning and Modernity: Religion, Polity, Self* (co-editor, 2003); *Popular China: Unofficial Culture in a Globalizing Society* (co-editor, 2002); *China's Catholics: Tragedy and Hope in an Emerging Civil Society* (1998); *China and the American Dream: A Moral Inquiry* (1995); and *The Good Society* (co-author, 1991).

Index